The Middle East

Other Books in the Current Controversies Series

The Middle East

Noël Merino, Book Editor

GREENHAVEN PRESS
A part of Gale, Cengage Learning

GALE
CENGAGE Learning·

Detroit • New York • San Francisco • New Haven, Conn • Waterville, Maine • London

Elizabeth Des Chenes, *Managing Editor*

For more information, contact:
Greenhaven Press
27500 Drake Rd.
Farmington Hills, MI 48331-3535
Or you can visit our Internet site at gale.cengage.com

For product information and technology assistance, contact us at

Gale Customer Support, 1-800-877-4253
For permission to use material from this text or product, submit all requests online at
www.cengage.com/permissions

Further permissions questions can be emailed to permissionrequest@cengage.com

Articles in Greenhaven Press anthologies are often edited for length to meet page requirements. In addition, original titles of these works are changed to clearly present the main thesis and to explicitly indicate the author's opinion. Every effort is made to ensure that Greenhaven Press accurately reflects the original intent of the authors. Every effort has been made to trace the owners of copyrighted material.

Cover image copyright © Jim Zuckerman/Corbis.

LIBRARY OF CONGRESS CATALOGING-IN-PUBLICATION DATA

The Middle East / Noël Merino, book editor.
    p. cm. -- (Current controversies)
    Includes bibliographical references and index.
    ISBN 978-0-7377-5628-9 (hardcover) -- ISBN 978-0-7377-5629-6 (pbk.)
    1. Middle East--Relations--United States. 2. United States--Relations--Middle East. 3. War on Terrorism, 2001-2009. 4. Iraq War, 2003- 5. Arab-Israeli conflict. I. Merino, Noël.
    DS63.2.U5M4733 2011
    956.05'4--dc23
                                      2011018847

Printed in the United States of America
1 2 3 4 5 6 7 15 14 13 12 11

Contents

Contrary to Iran's claim that its nuclear program is solely for civilian purposes, there is evidence that Iran has deceived the international community and could soon have nuclear weapons.

Chapter 2: How Can the Israeli-Palestinian Conflict Be Resolved?

Chapter 3: Have US Military Actions in the Middle East Been Effective?

Yes: US Military Actions in the Middle East Have Been Effective

The danger of an Iranian nuclear bomb, coupled with public opinion on the issue, supports the United States' using its military to destroy Iran's nuclear-weapon capacity.

No: The United States Should Not Be Involved with Problems in the Middle East

Foreword

By definition, controversies are "discussions of questions in which opposing opinions clash" (Webster's Twentieth Century Dictionary Unabridged). Few would deny that controversies are a pervasive part of the human condition and exist on virtually every level of human enterprise. Controversies transpire between individuals and among groups, within nations and between nations. Controversies supply the grist necessary for progress by providing challenges and challengers to the status quo. They also create atmospheres where strife and warfare can flourish. A world without controversies would be a peaceful world; but it also would be, by and large, static and prosaic.

The Series' Purpose

The purpose of the Current Controversies series is to explore many of the social, political, and economic controversies dominating the national and international scenes today. Titles selected for inclusion in the series are highly focused and specific. For example, from the larger category of criminal justice, Current Controversies deals with specific topics such as police brutality, gun control, white collar crime, and others. The debates in Current Controversies also are presented in a useful, timeless fashion. Articles and book excerpts included in each title are selected if they contribute valuable, long-range ideas to the overall debate. And wherever possible, current information is enhanced with historical documents and other relevant materials. Thus, while individual titles are current in focus, every effort is made to ensure that they will not become quickly outdated. Books in the Current Controversies series will remain important resources for librarians, teachers, and students for many years.

In addition to keeping the titles focused and specific, great care is taken in the editorial format of each book in the series. Book introductions and chapter prefaces are offered to provide background material for readers. Chapters are organized around several key questions that are answered with diverse opinions representing all points on the political spectrum. Materials in each chapter include opinions in which authors clearly disagree as well as alternative opinions in which authors may agree on a broader issue but disagree on the possible solutions. In this way, the content of each volume in Current Controversies mirrors the mosaic of opinions encountered in society. Readers will quickly realize that there are many viable answers to these complex issues. By questioning each author's conclusions, students and casual readers can begin to develop the critical thinking skills so important to evaluating opinionated material.

Current Controversies is also ideal for controlled research. Each anthology in the series is composed of primary sources taken from a wide gamut of informational categories including periodicals, newspapers, books, US and foreign government documents, and the publications of private and public organizations. Readers will find factual support for reports, debates, and research papers covering all areas of important issues. In addition, an annotated table of contents, an index, a book and periodical bibliography, and a list of organizations to contact are included in each book to expedite further research.

Perhaps more than ever before in history, people are confronted with diverse and contradictory information. During the Persian Gulf War, for example, the public was not only treated to minute-to-minute coverage of the war, it was also inundated with critiques of the coverage and countless analyses of the factors motivating US involvement. Being able to sort through the plethora of opinions accompanying today's major issues, and to draw one's own conclusions, can be a complicated and frustrating struggle. It is the editors' hope that Current Controversies will help readers with this struggle.

Introduction

"In many ways the notable features of the Middle East are at the core of what has created conflict in the Middle East for many decades."

The modern history of the Middle East began at the end of the nineteenth century when in 1869 the Suez Canal opened, providing a shortcut from the Mediterranean Sea to the Red Sea and the Indian Ocean. The Suez Canal connected the Middle East to the rest of the developing world, most notably bringing cultural, economic, and political contact with Europe and the United States. The modern Arab world began to take more distinct form after the fall of the Ottoman Empire in 1918. During World War I, Great Britain had promised to support Arab independence from the Ottomans in exchange for support during the war. Great Britain also was at the helm of the establishment of Israel, in the Balfour Declaration of 1917 stating the intent of "the establishment in Palestine of a national home for the Jewish people." Nations in the region moved toward independence after the fall of the Ottoman Empire, but the British and French had a strong presence in the region until after World War II.

The term "Middle East" gained traction after Captain Alfred Thayer Mahan, an American naval officer, used the term in a 1902 article to refer to the Persian Gulf region and southern Iran. Some claim that the term is Eurocentric, since it takes Europe as its starting point, with the Near East, Middle East, and Far East extending away from it. In addition to the debate about the relevance of the term, the exact geographical boundaries of the Middle East are not agreed upon and scholars disagree on what countries to include. Generally, the following countries are usually recognized as part of the Middle

East: Bahrain, Egypt, Iran, Iraq, Israel, Jordan, Kuwait, Lebanon, Oman, Qatar, Saudi Arabia, Syria, Turkey, United Arab Emirates, and Yemen.

Situated between the three continents of Africa, Asia, and Europe, what is notable about the fifteen countries of the Middle East is that they are primarily Arabic (with the notable exceptions of Iran, Israel, and Turkey) and Muslim (Israel being the most notable exception). In addition, a large number of Middle Eastern countries located around the Persian Gulf have economies that revolve around the production and export of petroleum—notably Saudi Arabia, Iran, United Arab Emirates, Kuwait, and Iraq.

In many ways the notable features of the Middle East are at the core of what has created conflict in the Middle East for many decades. The establishment of Israel, the world's only Jewish-majority state, in the middle of the Arab world has been a source of conflict since it officially declared independence in 1948. Support for Israel from the United States and Europe has created tensions between the Arab world and the West. Within the Muslim world, much conflict has occurred between the majority Sunnis of the region and the minority Shias. Throughout the Muslim countries, Islamic extremism has created challenges within the Middle East and with the international community. Finally, the vast profits to be made from Middle Eastern oil and its importance to countries around the world is also one of the reasons that this region is frequently a conflict area—both from within and from the outside.

In recent years there has been a tendency to include in the Middle East the countries of what is considered the Greater Middle East, especially those that share features with other Middle Eastern countries and those involved in neighboring conflicts with countries of the Middle East. To the south and west, the Arab League countries of northern Africa—Algeria, Djibouti, Libya, Mauritania, Morocco, Somalia, Sudan, and

Tunisia—are often said to be part of the Greater Middle East. To the north and east, the Greater Middle East is often noted as including the countries of Afghanistan, Armenia, Azerbaijan, Georgia, Kazakhstan, Kyrgyzstan, Pakistan, Tajikistan, Turkmenistan, and Uzbekistan.

The region of the Middle East is an area of several recent international wars, including the Iraq war and the ongoing war in Afghanistan. It is the site of the ongoing Israeli-Palestinian conflict, a battle that has raged for decades without lasting peace, despite many efforts by the international community to attempt to broker peace. The Greater Middle East is also home to numerous uprisings that began in 2011, including conflict in Bahrain, Egypt, Iraq, Libya, Saudi Arabia, Tunisia, and Yemen. The Middle East will likely be a region of conflict and concern for the international community for years to come, creating ongoing debate regarding how the United States and other countries should react. By presenting different viewpoints on the conflicts in the Middle East and possible resolutions, *Current Controversies: The Middle East* sheds light on the ongoing debates surrounding this volatile region of the world.

CHAPTER 1

What Are the Primary Concerns About the Middle East?

Chapter Preface

At the end of 2010, Mohamed Bouazizi, a Tunisian street vendor, set himself on fire in protest of alleged harassment by government officials in attempts to run his business. He died on January 4, 2011, setting off a wave of demonstrations and riots throughout the Greater Middle Eastern country of Tunisia. Tunisian protesters demanded reforms and elections in response to high unemployment, corruption, lack of freedom, and poor living conditions. On January 14, 2011, the protests culminated in the resignation of President Zine El Abidine Ben Ali, whose regime was considered by many to be undemocratic and authoritarian. The successful ousting of the Tunisian leader inspired similar opposition protests in other countries, including several self-immolations as acts of protest.

On Egypt's National Police Day, January 25, 2011, tens of thousands of Egyptian protesters took to the streets in several Egyptian cities, demanding resignation of President Hosni Mubarak. Similar to the protesters in Tunisia, Egyptian protesters expressed outrage at corruption and poor living conditions, but also demanded an end to police brutality. On February 11, 2011, Vice President Omar Suleiman announced that President Mubarak would step down after thirty years of autocratic rule.

In Yemen, the poorest country in the Arab world, protesters called for the resignation of President Ali Abdullah Saleh since January 2011. As of March 2011, the protests continued and government forces had killed and wounded numerous protesters.

In Bahrain, protests erupted to demand greater freedom and equality for the majority Shia Muslim population that is ruled by a Sunni Muslim minority headed by the King Hamad Bin Isa Al Khalifa. February 2011 protests led to ministerial changes and government promises to cancel some loans to citizens. Pro-democracy demonstrations continued, however, and in mid-March the monarchy responded by declaring martial law and aggressively clamping down on protesters.

Neighboring Saudi Arabia, also a monarchy, is an Islamic state ruled by the royal family Al Saud, headed by King Abdullah. Unlike Bahrain, however, both the monarchy and the vast majority of the general population are Sunni Muslim. Saudi Arabia sent troops to Bahrain in support of the king of Bahrain. Protests in Saudi Arabia have largely been defused by a huge police presence and an official ban on demonstrations. Protests by the minority Shia population in March 2011 were quieted with an offering by King Abdullah of $93 billion more in benefits to the people of this welfare state funded by oil profits.

In Libya, part of the Greater Middle East, antigovernment protests that began in February 2011 were met by military action authorized by Colonel Muammar al-Gaddafi. Gaddafi has been the leader of Libya since he led the military coup overthrowing King Idris in 1969. In response to the brutal military response by Gaddafi, the United Nations Security Council voted on March 17, 2011, to authorize military action against Gaddafi and the Libyan military that commenced immediately.

Elsewhere in the Middle East, there is unrest. In Iraq, protesters in early 2011 demanded better government services, with some violent clashes between protesters and police. In Jordan, King Abdullah II dismissed his cabinet and prime minister in January 2011 in an attempt to calm street protests. In Syria, protests began in March 2011, with Syrian demonstrators demanding release of political prisoners, more freedoms, and an end to pervasive corruption. It is too early to say what effect the political uprisings of 2011 will have on the Middle East. Even in countries such as Egypt where protesters were successful, it remains to be seen what reforms will be made and whether they will quell the conflict or increase it.

America's Reliance on Oil Funnels Money and Power to the Middle East

Gal Luft

Gal Luft is executive director of the Institute for the Analysis of Global Security (IAGS), a think tank focused on energy security, and coauthor of Turning Oil into Salt: Energy Independence Through Fuel Choice.

In the past half century, sharp increases in oil prices have been harbingers of most of America's economic recessions. Today is no exception: The quadrupling of oil prices in just six years [2002–2008] is a leading cause of America's current economic predicament. But in addition to the traditional dislocations associated with high oil prices, the current spike is also driving a structural shift in the world economic balance of power. Trillions of dollars are migrating from industrialized and developing nations to the coffers of a small group of oil-producing nations, most of them authoritarian and many of them unfriendly to the West. And unlike previous price spikes, this one is likely to last a long time, so it is high time that we think about the longer-term implications, and what to do about them.

An Economic Issue

For developing countries, many of which still carry debts from the oil shocks of the 1970s, $100-plus oil is in effect a regressive tax that slows economic growth and exacerbates existing social tensions. It also makes them economically and politically dependent on some of the world's nastiest petro-regimes. For the United States, with its net foreign debt in excess of $3 trillion and with oil spending at $1 billion per day, the current wealth transfer heralds geopolitical decline and eventual erosion of sovereignty in the form of lost control over major economic assets.

With annual oil revenues in excess of $1 trillion, the 13 members of the Organization of [the] Petroleum Exporting Countries (OPEC) already wield tremendous economic power. As recent multibillion-dollar bailouts of major financial institutions like Citigroup and Merrill Lynch show, these countries are not just laughing all the way to the bank; they now *own* the bank (or at least part of it, anyway). The bailout of America's prime symbols of economic prowess signals not only the vulnerability of the U.S. economy but also the ascent of sovereign wealth funds as new power brokers in international relations. These government-owned investment funds, whose combined assets currently surpass $3.5 trillion, are pouring billions into hedge funds, private equity funds, real estate, natural resources, media conglomerates and other nodes of the West's economy. Distressed financial institutions facing liquidity problems often find cash injections offered by sovereign wealth funds the only way to stay afloat.

Concern over Foreign Investors

Some experts dismiss the concern about foreign acquisitions of Western assets as a new form of jingoism. They deride the "fear mongers" as disciples of those who stoked the anti-Japanese hysteria of the 1980s. Sovereign wealth funds, they believe, are a boon to our economy, providing the capital and support for the tumbling dollar that holds back a financial meltdown of historic proportions. Furthermore, such rescue packages create an incentive for even the least friendly foreign governments to protect their investment by ensuring America's prosperity.

These claims may prove true if tensions between the United States and some of the investing countries eventually subside. If they do not, as is most likely, then soaking up Arab wealth (or Chinese, for that matter) could mean trouble, because there is a fundamental difference between state and private ownership. Lack of transparency allows many investor governments to blur the fine but clear line between government and private economic activity. Unlike ordinary shareholders and wealthy private investors who seek only profit, governments sometimes choose to maximize their geopolitical influence or promote anti-Western ideologies.

Perpetually high oil prices will undoubtedly transform the existing world economic order.

Of course, it depends on the state. Mitsubishi Estate, the Japanese company that caused an uproar when it bought Rockefeller Center in 1989, was not the Japanese government's handmaiden, and Japan was, and still is, an American ally. And Singapore, which recently promised the U.S. Treasury Secretary that it would not use its sovereign funds nest egg for political purposes, is also a friendly state that does not arouse much concern. The same can hardly be said about Russia, China or most OPEC members, some of which use their revenues to fund the proliferation of radical Islam, develop nuclear capabilities and serially violate human rights.

High Oil Prices

We dismiss this problem at our peril particularly because oil prices will not go down anytime soon. While OPEC governments enjoy wide and growing access to investment opportunities in the West, they have not reciprocated by opening their economies to foreign investment. On the contrary, they practice resource nationalism, stick to quotas and obstruct international companies from investing in their territories, limiting them to a minority share at best. This is one reason that Big Oil's access to equity oil and gas reserves has been in constant decline for decades, resulting in insufficient production of new oil. In the past decade, global oil demand grew by 11 million barrels per day, yet OPEC, which owns 77 percent of the world's reserves, contributed only half that amount.

Perpetually high oil prices will undoubtedly transform the existing world economic order, shifting the economic balance in OPEC's direction. Imagine, for instance that OPEC members are corporations and a barrel of oil is a share. At $100 per barrel of oil, OPEC's market capitalization, based on its proven reserves, stands at the time of this writing at roughly $92 trillion. This is about the total value of the world's stock and bond markets. Saudi Arabia's oil alone is worth $27 trillion, seven times the total value of all the companies traded in the London Stock Exchange. If one adds the worth of OPEC's huge gas reserves, as well as additional undiscovered oil reserves, OPEC's wealth more than doubles. If oil prices climb to $200 per barrel, as Venezuelan President Hugo Chávez recently warned they would, OPEC wealth will double again.

Current macroeconomic conditions clearly call for heightened vigilance.

Such monumental potential wealth enables a level of buying power that far eclipses that of the West. For instance, at $100 per barrel of oil OPEC could potentially buy the Bank of America with two months' worth of production, Apple Computers with two weeks' worth and General Motors with just six days' worth. It would take less than three years' worth of production for OPEC to own a 20 percent share of every S&P [Standard & Poor's] 500 company (enough to ensure a voting block in most corporations). Takeovers of such magnitude are unlikely in the foreseeable future, but what is clear about the new economic reality is that the economic power of America and its allies is constantly eroding as OPEC's "share" price is steadily rising.

The Buying Power from Oil

With soaring oil prices, Middle Eastern governments will have the ability to use their increased buying power as a means of extortion and overt intimidation whenever political differences emerge. This is all the more striking in light of the growing prospect of future bailouts in American sectors beyond banking—such as America's underfunded health care and retirement systems. The derivatives market, which has quintupled in the past five years, is another massive bubble waiting to explode—and potentially to be "saved" by OPEC state capital.

To date, the influx of petrodollars has not purchased too many seats for foreign agents in Western corporate boardrooms. That is because many of the sovereign wealth funds are prepared to forego board seats by buying holdings under the 5 percent benchmark that triggers regulatory scrutiny. But at the current rate of investment, and assuming several more years of high oil prices, some wealthy foreign governments might look to translate their wealth into power—by dictating business practices, vetoing deals, appointing officers sympathetic to their governments and dismissing those who are critical of them.

The gradual penetration of *sharia* [Islamic law] into the West's corporate world is another sign of our time. *Sharia* countries like Saudi Arabia have strict guidelines of economic conduct, such as prohibiting the collection and payment of interest and investments in businesses that sell unlawful products like alcohol and pork. Banks and investment houses are beginning to employ a new breed of executive, the chief *sharia* officer (CSO), whose sole job is to ensure compliance with Islamic law. Over time, such compliance could put pressure on companies at variance with Islamic principles to become more "Islamic." Imams sitting on *sharia* boards could be pressured to withhold their approval of any business dealing connected with countries or institutions that are offensive to Islam. The first signs of this can be seen in China, where pork, a food forbidden in Islam, is central to the cuisine. *Sharia*-compliant funds investing in commercial real estate force their tenants to limit the sale of pork and alcohol. "I need to go through each tenant's balance sheet to ensure that the non-*sharia* elements are at an acceptable level," said one Chinese trust manager.

Balancing Risks

Protecting America's economic sovereignty does not mean pulling up the drawbridge and isolating ourselves. America's commitment to open markets and the free flow of capital around the world has been a source of respect and admiration. Investment protectionism would hurt U.S. prestige while undermining economic growth and job creation at home. Nevertheless, we must strike a new balance, for current macroeconomic conditions clearly call for heightened vigilance.

A shift toward a global transportation system based on next-generation, nonpetroleum fuels should be America's top strategic economic priority.

The United States already has a rigorous safeguard mechanism to protect national security assets in sectors such as telecommunications, broadcasting, energy and minerals: the Committee on Foreign Investment in the United States (CFIUS). CFIUS has paid less attention to sectors with less obvious connections to national security, such as the auto industry. Yet sovereign funds have already put their sight on auto manufacturers, buying stakes in companies like Ferrari, Aston Martin and Daimler. In 2004 Abu Dhabi almost bought 25 percent of Volkswagen's shares after the German automaker's profits fell sharply. It is not unlikely that Arab sovereign wealth funds would be the first to step in to save the ailing U.S. auto industry from its massive pension obligations. What this might mean for U.S. efforts to make our cars less dependent on petroleum is a question policy makers should debate before such a crisis is upon them.

Adopting the principle of reciprocity is also an important step for policy makers to take. As mentioned, many of the countries investing in the West are notorious for their inhospitality to foreign investors and their egregious violations of free trade principles. The least we can do is demand that foreign nations treat us as we treat them. Despite being the leading violator of free trade by dint of its leadership of OPEC, Saudi Arabia was admitted to the World Trade Organization with U.S. support in 2005. This was a terrible blunder. Since their admission, the Saudis have responded to American generosity with nothing but continuous manipulation of oil prices. When President [George W.] Bush went to Riyadh [the capital of Saudi Arabia] in January 2008 to beg the Saudis to increase oil production, the Saudis announced that oil prices would remain "tied to market forces" (read: the whims of the OPEC cartel). When he went again this past May [2008], he got little more. The lesson here is that enjoying the benefits of free trade should be an earned privilege, not an entitlement, and foreign governments that wish to acquire assets in the West or seat their agents in Western boardrooms should be obliged to show similar hospitality to Western companies.

America's Top Priority

In the long run, the only way to roll back OPEC's influence, and with it Western vulnerability to potentially hostile use of sovereign wealth funds, is by reducing the strategic value of petroleum. The keys to this strategy are parked in our garages. Two-thirds of the oil the West uses is consumed in the transportation sector. Since the average life span of a car is nearly two decades, continuing to make cars that can run on nothing but petroleum recklessly locks our transportation sector to oil for the foreseeable future.

A shift toward a global transportation system based on next-generation, nonpetroleum fuels should be America's top strategic economic priority. The first step should be to ensure that every car put on the road is a flex-fuel car, which looks and operates exactly like a gasoline car but has a $100 feature that enables it to run on any combination of gasoline and alcohol.

Millions of flex-fuel cars on the road will ignite a boom of innovation and investment in alternative fuel technologies. The West is blessed with a wealth of affordable sources of alcohol fuels (ethanol and, better still, methanol). Among them are hundreds of years' worth of coal reserves, vast rich farmland and billions of tons per year of agricultural, industrial and municipal waste. (Remember that scene in one of the *Back to the Future* movies where the DeLorean retrofitted in the future is fueled from a neighbor's garbage? It was funny in the movie, but it may soon be no joke.) In an alcohol-fuel economy, scores of poor developing countries that now struggle with high oil prices would be able to excel as biomass-derived energy exporters, emerging as a powerful force in the global transportation sector.

It is in America's interest to help steer the wealth transfer inherent in high energy prices to countries that are friendlier and better behaved than those of the Middle East, Russia and Venezuela. Failure to do so will guarantee a metastasizing loss of sovereignty, economic and political decline, and a situation in which, in the words of the chief economist of the International Energy Agency, "we are ending up with 95 percent of the world relying for its economic well-being on decisions made by five or six countries in the Middle East."

Palestinian Reluctance to Accept the Jewish State Makes Peace Impossible

David Frum

David Frum is the editor of FrumForum.com and a former special assistant to President George W. Bush.

To understand the challenge of the Middle East peace process, try this analogy: Imagine you are a conscientious, intelligent official in your state's highway department. The public complains that suburban roads are becoming intensely overcrowded. Voters demand you widen the roads to relieve congestion.

A Futile Cycle

Now you know perfectly well that road-widening is useless. Long experience has taught you that when the state widens roads, it only invites more commercial development along the roads. New development encourages more traffic, and soon the congestion has clogged more than ever.

The real answer is radically different: more mass transit, different kinds of zoning, etc. The trouble is, you work in the highway department. You have no control over any of those things. The only thing you can do is build roads. So, in full awareness of the pointlessness—indeed the total counterproductivity—of the exercise, you do the one thing you can do. You widen the road.

Israeli-Palestinian negotiations are trapped in the same futile cycle. They don't work. But the things that might work are not typically included in the remit of the peace processors.

The "peace process" is bilateral; the peace problem is regional. The "peace process" is concerned with boundaries between Israel and Palestine; the peace problem is concerned with the unwillingness of Israel's Arab neighbors to accept the Jewish state as a permanent fact. The "peace process" is diplomatic; the peace problem is cultural, ideological and religious.

It's hard to criticize the peace processors. They are inspired by some of the best values in Western culture generally and American politics specifically. They believe in focusing on limited, solvable issues. They believe in compromise and negotiation. They believe that coexistence is the natural state of affairs, and that conflict is abnormal.

They are reasonable people, but they are engaged in an unreasonable task. Yet they return again and again to the hopeless spiral. Even the names are unchanged: Dennis Ross, George Mitchell, and all the other envoys, ambassadors, rapporteurs and plenipotentiaries.

Complexity and Conflict

It's often said that the Middle East peace process is very complicated. That's not exactly true. The tax treaty between Canada and the United States: That's complicated. The federal-state tax treatment of undistributed timber royalties alone is enough to crack the jaw. But nobody is detonating bombs over Canada-U.S. timber taxes.

Managing cooperative relationships like those between Canada and the United States is complex, because cooperation creates ramifying connections and relationships that demand ever more elaborate governance. Conflict, by contrast, is not complicated. Two parties want the same thing—and only one can have it. The Israeli-Palestinian conflict is even simpler, because very often the only reason that something has value in Palestinian eyes is precisely in order to deny it to the Israelis. Daniel Pipes has demonstrated this point very learnedly in the case of the holy sites of Jerusalem: Through most of the past

1,300 years, Muslims have attached very little value to those sites. They become important only when anybody else gains possession of them. Only in three brief periods of contestation—the 7th century, the 12th, and now the 21st—has the city been felt to matter. When Muslim sovereignty was regained, the city was forgotten.

A British official who worked on the Irish peace process told me that the process really took hold when people from both sides sat down and listened with some understanding to the narrative told by the other—when Sinn Féin could acknowledge the Unionists' view of history, and the Unionists could recognize Sinn Féin's. They did not have to agree with each other, but they had to abide each other.

The Palestinian and Israeli Narratives

Israelis and western Jews have generally had little difficulty recognizing—if not accepting—the Palestinian narrative. There's no Israeli equivalent of the attempts to deny, not just the Holocaust, but the existence of Herod's Temple [part of a Jewish holy site in Jerusalem] or the Maccabean commonwealth [Jewish inhabitants of Jerusalem in the 1st and 2nd centuries].

Equal recognition of the Israeli narrative, however, is adamantly repudiated by Palestinians. Look at the Clinton/Arafat/Barak [referring to President Bill Clinton, Palestinian leader Yasser Arafat, and Israeli Prime Minister Ehud Barak] peace negotiations of 1999–2001. They did not break down over water rights or work permits. They broke down over moral issues: the Palestinian demands for a so-called "right of return" into Israel, for exclusive jurisdiction over the holy sites of Jerusalem and for some monetary act of atonement from Israel. It is striking how many of these demands are mimicked from Israel's history; the right of return from Israeli law, the monetary compensation from West Germany's payments to the Jewish state after World War II.

The trouble is that so long as the Palestinians signal their repudiation of Israel's legitimacy, Israel must in turn impose stringent security conditions upon any Palestinian government: demilitarization, policing by NATO [North Atlantic Treaty Organization] or some other international organization and prohibition of any military alliance with other regional states. Under these conditions, an independent Palestine would begin to look more like a Vatican City autonomous region than a full-fledged state.

Palestinians resent and reject such supervision. But failing an internal commitment to live in peace, such external conditions become inescapable. The Prussian military theorist Carl von Clausewitz famously observed that in war, everything is very simple, but the simplest things are extremely hard. So it is in the Middle East. And the effort to circumvent those difficulties by focusing on other things—Israeli settlements, for example—only plunges us into the same hopeless repetition as a state's attempt to pave its way out of traffic congestion.

The Lack of an Independent Palestinian State Makes Peace Impossible

Mustafa Barghouthi

Mustafa Barghouthi is a physician and an advocate for the development of Palestinian civil society and grassroots democracy. He was a candidate for the presidency of the Palestinian National Authority in 2005, finishing second.

Negotiations between two unequal parties cannot succeed. Success in Palestinian-Israeli negotiations requires a reasonable balance of power, clear terms of reference and abstention of both sides from imposing unilateral facts on the ground. None of that existed in the talks that were re-initiated in September.

Much like previous rounds of talks, these negotiations were dominated on one side by an Israeli government that controls the land, roads, airspace, borders, water and electricity, as well as the trade and economy of the Palestinian side, while possessing a powerful military establishment (now the third military exporter in the world) and a robust gross domestic product, which has tripled in the last decade.

This same Israeli "partner" now also boasts a general public that has shifted dramatically to the right, and to which an apartheid system for Palestinians has become an acceptable norm.

On the other side is the Palestinian Authority—one that paradoxically holds little real authority, and exists as a sort of fiefdom within the Israeli matrix of control. Further debilitating the P.A. is a protracted internal Palestinian division, total dependence on foreign aid and a decline of democracy and human rights. Finally, the Palestinian Authority is constantly pressured to provide security for its occupier while failing to provide any protection whatsoever to its own people from that same occupier.

How did we get here? The answer, in large part, has to do with the continued and unabated construction of settlements in the West Bank and East Jerusalem in the 17 years since the Oslo agreement.

In this time, the number of settlers has increased by 300 percent and the number of settlements has doubled. The settlements are only the front line of a complex and profitable system that includes checkpoints, road segregation, security zones, the "apartheid wall" and "natural reserves."

This matrix has for years eaten up the land, water resources and the economic space of the independent Palestinian state supposedly being negotiated in this same period. About 60 percent of the West Bank and 80 percent of water resources have been consumed this way.

We have reached, and probably surpassed, that critical point at which any more settlements mean the death of the two-state solution.

The Israeli establishment knows this better than anybody. They also know that their hard-line positions on issues like Jerusalem and borders mean transforming the idea of Palestinian statehood into something much less: isolated clusters of land in a system of segregation.

The International Court of Justice and endless United Nations resolutions have ruled that settlements are illegal and should be removed. Even the Road Map issued by the so-called Quartet (the United States, the United Nations, the European Union and Russia) in 2003 said that all settlement activities must stop. Yet neither the United States nor the Quartet as a whole has had the guts to exert serious pressure on Israel to stop settlements.

So what is left?

The only way to save the two-state solution is for the Palestinians to declare the establishment of an independent Palestinian state on the territories occupied by Israel in 1967, including East Jerusalem, and to demand that the world community recognize it and its borders—as it did in the case of Kosovo.

That would also mean supporting the right of Palestinians to struggle nonviolently to end the occupation of their state. Any future negotiations, therefore, would not be about the right of the Palestinians to have their own sovereign independent state, but rather about how to apply and implement that right.

This would be the true test of the state-building strategy of the United States and the donor community. It would be the real instrument to finally demarcate the difference between support for free Palestinian institutions in a sovereign and viable state, or footing the bill of occupation and using E.U. and U.S. tax dollars to maintain under various guises what will never amount to anything but an apartheid system denying Palestinians their human and national rights.

If the world community turns its back on such a declaration of independence by using the well-worn and insulting argument that every step should first be verified with the Israeli government, then the message will be clear: Peace based on two states is no longer an option.

Ethnic Tensions in Iraq Make Long-Term Stability in the Region Unlikely

Ted Galen Carpenter

Ted Galen Carpenter is the vice president for defense and foreign policy studies at the Cato Institute and author of Smart Power: Toward a Prudent Foreign Policy for America.

The United States seems committed to drawing down its forces in Iraq, with the goal of having all combat forces out of the country by the end of 2011. That is also the wish of Prime Minister Nouri al-Maliki's government and a majority of the Iraqi people. The first step in that process was the withdrawal of US troops from Iraq's cities (with the exception of Mosul, where the antigovernment insurgency remains potent) by 30 June 2009. It was a disturbing development, though, that a noticeable spike in violence occurred as the US forces redeployed and turned security responsibilities over to Iraqi military and police units.

Experts both in the United States and in Iraq worry that the relative calm that Iraq has enjoyed since mid-2007 might not last once US troops depart. Indeed, there are serious questions about whether Iraq can be a viable state over the long run. If Iraq becomes a cockpit of instability again, as it was during the first four years following the US invasion, the implications for the region are ominous. Unfortunately, the factors that might cause the country to unravel are largely beyond the control of the United States. In fact, the US ouster of Saddam Hussein and the long-governing Sunni elite was the catalyst that unleashed many of those forces.

Ted Galen Carpenter, "Middle East Vortex: An Unstable Iraq and Its Implications for the Region," *Mediterranean Quarterly*, vol. 20, no. 4, Fall 2009, pp. 22–31. Copyright © 2009 Mediterranean Affairs, Inc. All rights reserved. Reprinted by permission of the publisher, Duke University Press.

The Issue of Kurdistan

In one sense, Iraq has already ceased to be a unified state. The Baghdad [capital of Iraq] government plays no meaningful role in the Kurdish region in the north. Indeed, Iraqi Arabs who enter the territory are treated as foreigners—and not especially welcome foreigners. Officially, Kurdistan is merely a region of Iraq that Baghdad allows to exercise "autonomy," but Iraqi Kurdistan has its own government, flag, national anthem, currency, and army (the Peshmerga). The flag issue is particularly revealing. Even though Kurdistan is supposedly part of Iraq, it was illegal there to fly the Iraqi flag until early 2008, and such displays are discouraged even today. When Kurdish officials speak publicly, they typically refer to their area as merely a self-governing region of Iraq, but when they speak privately, that cover story often disappears. With the Kurdish population, there is seldom even the pretense of an allegiance to Iraq. Media interviews and opinion surveys show overwhelming majorities in favor of full-fledged independence.

Although the Kurds have not proclaimed an independent country, in every sense that matters Iraq's Kurdistan region is *de facto* [in practice] independent, and the "Kurdish regional government" is the governing body of a sovereign state. Moreover, it is a *de facto* sovereign state with far-reaching territorial goals. Within Iraq, the Kurds claim the northern city of Kirkuk and its extensive oil deposits. There have also been nasty clashes with Iraqi Arab factions in the ethnically mixed province of Nineveh, where Kurds insist that several villages should be part of the Kurdish region.

Thanks to US assistance, Kurdistan has enjoyed *de facto* independence since the end of the Persian Gulf War in 1991. When Washington began to enforce a no-fly zone over northern Iraq, the Kurds took advantage of that protection to establish and consolidate their region's self-rule. Unable to bring his air power to bear, Saddam Hussein could not reassert

Baghdad's control, since the Peshmerga was more than a match for Iraqi ground forces. More recently, the Peshmerga have been strong enough to prevent infiltration by al Qaeda or Iraqi Arab Sunni and Shiite militias.

That relatively stable security environment has enabled Kurdistan to enjoy solid economic growth—in contrast to the rather dismal situation in the rest of Iraq. A construction boom has taken place in Kurdish cities, and Western firms in an assortment of industries seem eager to invest in Kurdistan. The current global economic recession has slowed the process, but just modestly. Foreign investment interest is most pronounced with regard to Kurdish oil production, but it extends to other economic arenas as well. It is especially revealing that companies wishing to do business in Kurdistan normally work through the regional government, not Baghdad. Despite vehement complaints from Iraqi leaders (and US occupation authorities), the Kurdish government continues to sign multimillion-dollar agreements with various Western companies. In addition, Iraqi Kurdistan is building its own oil refineries, a step that gives it further independence from Baghdad on energy issues.

The potential for a major dust-up with Turkey over the PKK is not the only situation in which Kurdistan could be the catalyst for a regional crisis.

The Kurds and Turkey

Despite its economic and political achievements, there is almost no prospect for international recognition of an independent Kurdistan. Washington opposes such a step, fearing that proclaiming Kurdish independence would not only lead to further fragmentation of Iraq but would antagonize all of Iraqi Kurdistan's neighbors, especially Turkey. That is a legitimate concern. The underlying problem is that the Kurds are the largest nationality in the world without an officially recognized state. Although the British government promised the Kurds a homeland following the wreckage of the Ottoman Empire after World War I, London reneged on that commitment, and Kurdish territory was divided among Iraq, Iran, Syria, and Turkey. Any talk of an independent Kurdistan sets off alarm bells in Tehran, Damascus, and especially Ankara [the capitals of Iran, Syria, and Turkey respectively], since fully 50 percent of Kurds live in Turkey.

Ankara is already less than pleased with the existence of a *de facto* Kurdish state in Iraq. And Turkish leaders have reason to be uneasy. The Turkish military has waged a war for some two-and-a-half decades against Kurdish secessionists, led by the Kurdistan Workers' Party (PKK). Fighting flared during 2007, with PKK fighters striking targets inside Turkey and then taking refuge across the border in Iraqi Kurdistan. Ankara's patience finally ran out in late 2007, and Turkish military forces launched attacks on some of those sanctuaries. Turkey had actually threatened a much larger operation, and Washington feared that the incursions could lead to a full-scale war between Turkish military units and the Peshmerga. US officials prevailed upon Ankara to limit its military operations in exchange for US intelligence and other assistance against the PKK and a commitment from Iraqi Kurdish leaders to take action against PKK activities in their territory.

The situation became especially tense when Turkey delayed withdrawing its forces until March 2008. There were also indications that those troops were targeting Iraqi Kurdish installations as well as PKK enclaves, and at one point Kurdish Peshmerga forces surrounded a Turkish unit and threatened to open fire. After the Turkish withdrawal, angry Iraqi Kurds vowed to fight any future incursion—creating the prospect of a collision, since Ankara stated that its troops would return if the PKK establishes bases in Iraqi Kurdistan from which to attack targets inside Turkey.

The City of Kirkuk

The potential for a major dust-up with Turkey over the PKK is not the only situation in which Kurdistan could be the catalyst for a regional crisis. Another flash point involves the future political status of the city of Kirkuk and its oil riches. Kirkuk is an ethnically mixed city of Arabs, Kurds, and Turkmen (kinsmen that Turkey has pledged to protect). During Saddam Hussein's rule, Baghdad pursued a blatant policy of Arabization, expelling Kurdish families and replacing them with Arabs. Since his overthrow, that process has been reversed, with Kurdish authorities expelling Arabs (and some Turkmen) and Kurds moving in.

The Kurdistan government keeps pressing for a referendum among voters in Kirkuk on the city's political status, with the goal of incorporating it into Kurdistan's jurisdiction. That referendum, which the Iraqi central government originally promised to hold before the end of 2007, has been repeatedly postponed—much to the annoyance of Kurdish authorities. It will not be possible to avoid that issue forever, though.

The government in Baghdad understandably worries about losing the revenue from Kirkuk's oil.

Kurdish officials seem to be running out of patience and have begun to take a harder line on Kirkuk and other matters. Regional president Masoud Barzani spurned a UN [United Nations] proposal to resolve the contentious internal border disputes. The principal option pushed by UN officials was to make Kirkuk province into an autonomous region—not under the direct control of either the Baghdad government or the Kurdish regional government. American officials have repeatedly expressed support for a UN-brokered solution.

Barzani has no patience for such a scheme. Indeed, the Kurdish government is moving decisively in the opposite direction. In June 2009, the region's parliament approved a draft constitution that extended Kurdish political and economic rights to all disputed territories, including Kirkuk. That constitutional provision asserted unequivocally that the disputed territories are inseparable from the "geographic and historic entity" today known as Iraq's Kurdistan region. Barzani also issued a chilling warning: "If any regional country, or even Baghdad, interferes in an internal matter, and individuals inside the region conspire against the region's security and well-being," he stressed, "actions will be taken in accordance with the law against those who want to undermine the unity of the Kurdish house."

Whatever the result of the referendum on Kirkuk when it is finally held, there is likely to be trouble. If the Kurds lose, the resulting anger throughout Kurdistan would probably eradicate any lingering facade of loyalty to the Iraqi state. But given the ongoing ethnic cleansing, the Kurds are almost certain to win, and that result would have explosive potential on multiple fronts.

Opposition to a Kurdistan Kirkuk

The government in Baghdad understandably worries about losing the revenue from Kirkuk's oil. Both Shiite and Sunni Arab leaders also suspect that a Kurdish regional government with a dramatically enhanced source of revenue would be even more inclined to pursue independent policies on a wide range of issues. Kurdish-Arab tensions have already grown so severe that Secretary of Defense Robert Gates made an unexpected trip to Iraq to urge both sides to back away from a dangerous confrontation. General Ray Odierno, the top US commander in Iraq, admitted that the Arab-Kurdish feud—especially over the status of Kirkuk—is the "number one driver of instabilities" in the country. Tensions in both the area around Kirkuk and in Nineveh province became so pronounced in August 2009 that Odierno suggested that US troops be deployed to create a buffer between Kurds and Arabs to prevent an explosion.

Turkey is agitated about the prospect that its Turkmen brethren might become an even more discriminated against minority than they are now. Even more important, Ankara fears that control of Kirkuk's oil wealth would enable Kurdistan to become a major economic and political player in the region and allow Kurdish leaders to cast off all pretenses that Kurdistan is anything other than an independent state. Such an entity, Turkish officials worry, would be an irresistible magnet for Turkey's own restless Kurdish minority and risk fragmenting the country. Ankara has repeatedly indicated that it might take forcible action if Kirkuk is incorporated into Kurdistan.

Iraq is still in the throes of a civil war, albeit a relatively low-intensity one.

To make matters even more volatile, Kurdistan's own political stability is less certain today than it was in previous years. A new party, Goran (Change), cut into the dominance long exercised by the two major parties, the Patriotic Union of Kurdistan (PUK) and the Kurdish Democratic Party (KDP), winning more than a quarter of the vote in the July 2009 elections. Among other effects, that outcome may cause both the PUK and the KDP to intensify their appeal to Kurdish nationalist sentiments as a way to prevent further erosion of their political strength. A key plank in Goran's platform was that the two leading parties had done a poor job of standing up for Kurdish interests in dealing with the Baghdad government. In any case, the positions adopted by the Kurdish regional government are no longer as predictable as they were under the stable political duopoly that existed before the July vote.

A Continued Civil War

In addition to the fracture of Iraq caused by the existence of a *de facto* independent Kurdish state with ambitious territorial claims, there are serious questions about the degree of stability in the rest of Iraq. True, the carnage that afflicted the country following the US invasion, and which reached especially severe levels from early 2006 to mid-2007, has declined. Nevertheless, the casualty rates are still disturbingly high. Al Qaeda in Iraq, while weakened, remains a factor, and nervous Iraqi and US officials see indications that terrorist fighters are returning to some of their old haunts. The indigenous Sunni insurgency against the Shiite-dominated government also remains a worry. And general Shiite-Sunni sectarian tensions simmer just beneath the surface—a situation that continues to worry [Barack] Obama administration officials, in addition to their concerns about the growing Kurdish-Arab animosity.

Even the improvement in the casualty numbers should not be overstated. According to Iraq's Ministry of the Interior, there were 437 deaths in July, and another 1,103 Iraqis were wounded. Both totals were a decline from the upward trend in casualties that occurred during the first half of 2009 (including 543 deaths in June). The killings are dramatically lower (by about 75 percent) than they were during the horrid period in 2006 and 2007, but Iraq is still far from being a safe and peaceful country. Given that Iraq's population is only 25 million, even the July toll would translate into an equivalent of more than five thousand deaths from political violence in the United States—an annual rate of more than sixty thousand. Iraq is still in the throes of a civil war, albeit a relatively low-intensity one. That does not bode well for unity or even stability going forward.

A major reason for the decline in casualties since the summer of 2007 was the decision by then US military commander General David Petraeus to try to split indigenous Iraqi Sunnis from their al Qaeda allies. He did so by reaching out to—and generously funding—new Awakening Councils. Indeed, the US military provided weapons as well as money to those groups, despite uneasiness on the part of the Maliki regime. As the United States has begun to draw down its forces and reduce its overall role in Iraq, however, Shiite hard-liners in the Baghdad government have begun to harass the Awakening Councils. In late March 2009, government security forces even arrested prominent Awakening Council leaders—an action that produced a sharp increase in tensions and a scrambling US effort to mediate the dispute.

There is a significant chance that the already frosty relationship between Baghdad and the Awakening Councils will worsen once the United States completes its withdrawal. It is not even out of the question that full-scale sectarian fighting could erupt again. The continuing Shiite-Sunni rivalry also has regional implications. Before the Petraeus initiative, Iran and Saudi Arabia were at least mildly engaged in a proxy struggle in Iraq. The Saudis, with the blessing if not the active support of the royal family, supplied Iraqi Sunni militias with funds and weapons.

Iran's Influence in Iraq

Shiite Iran played a more complex game, working to establish reasonably cooperative ties with the Maliki government while providing some financial and logistical support for more radical Shiite factions. That strategy appears to have paid significant political dividends for Tehran. A graphic symbol of Iran's prestige and influence in Iraq came in March 2008 when Iranian president Mahmoud Ahmadinejad received an enthusiastic, red-carpet reception in Baghdad. In September 2007, President George W. Bush also visited Iraq, entering the country at a US military base in Anbar province with no advance public announcement. The contrast between those two visits could not have provided a clearer indication of which country was likely to have the greater long-term influence in Iraq.

The extent of the cordial ties between Baghdad and Tehran became even more apparent in the summer of 2009. Iraqi officials were noticeably quiet about the political turmoil in their eastern neighbor following Iran's disputed presidential election. American officials who thought that Iraqi democrats might back Iranian reformers against Ahmadinejad and the Islamic hard-liners were soon disappointed. Both Iraq's Shiite clerics and government officials provided virtually no support, even rhetorical, for the demonstrators. A short time later, Iraqi military forces moved to shut down the camp of a major Iranian exile group, the Mujahideen-e-Khalq, apparently at Tehran's request. The Iraqi government did not even inform the United States of that planned crackdown.

Iraq is the vortex in a turbulent part of the world.

It is apparent that Iran's influence in Iraq has grown dramatically since the ouster of Saddam Hussein, and Tehran will not willingly relinquish that status. It is also apparent that the neighboring Sunni powers, especially Saudi Arabia and Kuwait, are not at all happy about Iran's ascendency. The potential exists for a nasty Sunni-Shiite proxy struggle with Iraq as the main arena.

The Role of the United States

Given the Kurdish-Arab tensions in Iraq, the uneasy relations—to put it mildly—between Iraqi Kurdistan and neighboring states, simmering Sunni-Shiite tensions within Iraq, and the potential for a regional Sunni-Shiite proxy fight, the long-term prognosis for Iraq and regional stability is not good. Indeed, we may come to regard the period between mid-2007 and mid-2009 as a relatively quiet interlude between two turbulent and violent periods. Some members of the foreign policy community fear precisely that kind of outcome, and they advocate that the Obama administration abandon, or at least postpone, its plans to withdraw US forces from Iraq by the end of 2011.

Their diagnosis may well be correct, but their policy prescription is both futile and dangerous. The United States has already lost more than forty-three hundred troops (plus thousands more seriously wounded) and spent nearly $700 billion in direct expenditures in its nation-building venture. Yet crucial systemic and structural factors make it unlikely that Iraq will ever be a stable, united, democratic country. Proponents of keeping US troops in Iraq indefinitely would simply have America spend even more blood and treasure in pursuit of an unattainable objective. The unpleasant reality is that, regardless of when American forces leave Iraq, both that country and the wider region are probably in for a nasty period of instability. Iraq is the vortex in a turbulent part of the world, and there is little the United States can do to prevent its destructive impact.

Iran Is Making
Progress on the Acquisition
of Nuclear Weapons

James Phillips

James Phillips is the senior research fellow for Middle Eastern affairs at the Douglas and Sarah Allison Center for Foreign Policy Studies at the Heritage Foundation.

Iran's hard-line President Mahmoud Ahmadinejad celebrated the anniversary of Iran's 1979 revolution on February 11 [2010] by proclaiming that Iran is a "nuclear state." Iran's radical Shia Islamist regime clearly sees its nuclear program as a means of bolstering its sagging legitimacy and popularity, while expanding its prestige and global influence. It also sees nuclear weapons as a potent equalizer that could deter external attack and ensure its own survival. Tehran [Iran's capital] has spurned aggressive diplomatic offers from the [Barack] Obama administration to resolve the outstanding nuclear issue, just as it spurned efforts by the [George W.] Bush administration and by Britain, France, and Germany. As Ahmadinejad said in 2007, Iran's nuclear program is like a train "with no brakes and no reverse gear." Despite five U.N. [United Nations] Security Council resolutions and three rounds of U.N. sanctions, Iran's nuclear train speeds onward.

A Lack of Cooperation from Iran

Iran has forged ahead on its nuclear program despite growing international pressure to comply with its nuclear safeguard agreement with the International Atomic Energy Agency (IAEA). Since the discovery of its secret uranium enrichment facility at Natanz in 2002, Tehran has failed to keep its repeated pledges to cooperate fully with the IAEA to demonstrate that it has not used its civilian nuclear program as a fig leaf to mask a nuclear weapons program. Tehran has refused to fully disclose its nuclear activities and to stop its uranium enrichment efforts, which can produce fuel for nuclear reactors or, with further enrichment, the fissile material for a nuclear weapon. Iran has also pushed ahead on its ballistic missile program and building a nuclear warhead that can be delivered by a missile.

The Obama administration has sought to engage Iran diplomatically to defuse the nuclear standoff, but with little success. Instead, over the past year [2009–2010], Iran has spurned Western proposals to resolve the nuclear issue, insisted that it will continue to expand its nuclear program, installed hundreds more centrifuges to enrich uranium, been caught secretly constructing another uranium enrichment facility, and pledged to build 10 more.

Moreover, on December 14, 2009, the *Times* of London reported that Western intelligence agencies had uncovered Iranian documents indicating that Iranian scientists had tested a neutron initiator, the component that triggers a nuclear weapon. A neutron initiator has no peaceful application. This discovery directly contradicts the U.S. intelligence community's position that Iran halted nuclear weapons–related work in 2003. On December 18, Iran announced that it was testing more advanced centrifuges, which could enrich uranium faster.

A More Objective Look

Since 2002, the IAEA has bent over backwards to give Iran the benefit of the doubt, in large part due to the politicized leadership of IAEA Director General Mohamed ElBaradei, who was an outspoken critic of the Bush administration and often acted as an apologist for Iran. In November 2009, ElBaradei was replaced by Yukiya Amano of Japan.

Under Director General Amano's leadership, the IAEA appears to be taking a more objective look at the Iranian nuclear program. On February 18, it issued a confidential report that warned for the first time of evidence that Tehran is working on a nuclear warhead for its missiles. This warning contradicts the controversial 2007 U.S. National Intelligence Estimate (NIE), which concluded that Iran had stopped working on a nuclear weapon in 2003.

It is time for the Obama administration to acknowledge that its engagement policy has failed to budge the dictatorship in Tehran on the nuclear issue or on any other issue. As the history of Iran's nuclear program makes clear, Tehran has resisted multiple opportunities to defuse mounting tensions over its nuclear program.

Tehran claims that Iran's nuclear program is devoted solely to civilian nuclear power and research purposes. This contention is contradicted by many facts and by a series of recent revelations.

The Iranian nuclear program cannot be justified on strictly economic or energy grounds.

Evidence Disputing a Civilian Program

Fact #1: Iran has built an extensive and expensive nuclear infrastructure that is much larger than what would be necessary to support a civilian nuclear power program.

Iran's nuclear weapons program, cloaked within its civilian nuclear power program, has made steady advances. Iran operates a large uranium enrichment facility at Natanz, which it illegally sought to conceal until 2003, and it is building up a stockpile of enriched uranium that is of no current use in its civilian nuclear energy program. Iran's only nuclear power plant, which Russian technicians have almost finished testing at Bushehr, does not need domestically produced nuclear fuel because Moscow has agreed to provide all the enriched uranium that Iran needs to operate it for the first 10 years of operation. Moreover, Iran does not have a fuel fabrication plant that can produce reactor fuel for the Bushehr facility.

Iran has pursued virtually every possible technology for producing nuclear fuel and did so covertly and in violation of its treaty obligations to keep the IAEA informed. This includes laser separation, a costly and complex technology to enrich uranium that is ill suited to producing fissile fuel for a reactor. Iran has also conducted plutonium experiments and is building a reactor that appears intended for the large-scale production of plutonium.

Iran has a long record of denial and deceit on the nuclear issue.

The Iranian nuclear program cannot be justified on strictly economic or energy grounds. Iran lacks sufficient uranium reserves to run power reactors for more than 10 years and would eventually be forced to import either uranium yellowcake or finished fuel rods to operate them. Moreover, harnessing Iran's enormous natural gas reserves to generate electricity would be far less expensive, given that Iran is currently flaring and burning off natural gas as a by-product of oil production. . . .

Fact #2: Iran sought to buy technology from A. Q. [Abdul Qadeer] Khan's nuclear weapon proliferation network, which also provided assistance to Libya and North Korea.

Concrete evidence has confirmed long-held suspicions that Iran advanced its nuclear weapons program in close cooperation with A. Q. Khan's proliferation network, which dealt in weapons-related nuclear technologies. After initially denying this cooperation, Tehran eventually admitted that it had contacts with the network, but maintains that it broke off contact long ago.

Khan, the father of Pakistan's nuclear weapons program, has proudly admitted his role in helping Iran's nuclear program. He admitted in a televised interview in August 2009 that he and other senior Pakistani officials had helped to advance Iran's nuclear weapons program. If Iran's nuclear efforts were exclusively focused on civilian uses, as it maintains, it would have had no reason to collude with A. Q. Khan's nuclear smuggling operation, which specialized in the proliferation of nuclear weapons technologies.

Evidence of Deceit

Fact #3: Iran continues to conceal and lie about its nuclear weapons efforts.

Iran has a long record of denial and deceit on the nuclear issue. The Iranian regime ordered covert research and development on nuclear weapons and built secret pilot projects on uranium conversion and uranium enrichment in violation of its safeguards agreement with the IAEA, and it lied about these activities for years. In 2003, after the U.S. military overthrew Saddam Hussein's regime in neighboring Iraq, in part because of Hussein's lack of cooperation with U.N. inspectors, Iran admitted some of these activities and agreed to cooperate more fully with the IAEA investigators. However, Tehran reneged on its promise to cooperate and reverted to a hard-line policy after Mahmoud Ahmadinejad became president in 2005.

Today, Iran continues to stonewall IAEA efforts to investigate its suspect nuclear program. It refuses to answer questions about the mounting evidence of its past nuclear weapons development efforts, contending that documents indicating that it has carried out weapons design and testing work are forgeries. It has illegally neglected its treaty obligations to provide advance notice of new nuclear facilities and allow IAEA inspectors to have regular access to facilities under construction. The IAEA has also discovered that Tehran engaged in clandestine nuclear activities that violated its nuclear safeguards agreement, such as plutonium separation experiments, uranium enrichment and conversion experiments, and importing uranium compounds.

Iran continues to play a cat and mouse game with IAEA inspectors by hiding facilities, equipment, and materials from them and by refusing to give them timely access to other facilities. In September, Tehran was forced to admit the existence of a clandestine uranium enrichment facility near the city of Qom. President Barack Obama announced its discovery shortly after Western intelligence agencies had identified it. . . .

Fact #4: Iran rejected a nuclear deal that would have advanced its civilian nuclear efforts, belying its claims that civilian purposes are its only motivation.

Tehran has walked away from an offer brokered by the IAEA to enrich Iranian uranium in facilities outside Iran to refuel the Tehran Research Reactor. On October 1, 2009, Iran reached an "agreement in principle" at the Geneva talks that would have sent roughly 80 percent of Iran's LEU [low-enriched uranium] stockpile to Russia for processing and then to France for fabrication into fuel rods. The uranium would then be returned to Iran to power its research reactor, which will run out of fuel at the end of 2010. This deal would have benefited Iran by extending the operational life of its Tehran Research Reactor and aiding hundreds of thousands of medical patients. It would also have temporarily defused the nuclear standoff by reducing Iran's steadily growing LEU stockpile and postponing Iran's ability to build a nuclear weapon.

After reaching the agreement in principle, the Iranian regime backpedaled and made an unacceptable counterproposal in mid-December that would have greatly reduced the amount of uranium that would leave Iran. U.S. officials say that Ahmadinejad initially accepted the deal, but was rebuked by Iranian Supreme Leader Ayatollah Ali Khamenei and pulled back from it. On November 3, Ayatollah Khamenei warned Iranian political leaders to be wary of dealings with the United States, which could not be trusted, and said that negotiating with the United States was "naïve and perverted."

The Iranian regime's initial acceptance and subsequent rejection of the nuclear deal is consistent with its long-established pattern of cheat, retreat, and delay on nuclear issues. When caught cheating on its nuclear safeguards obligations, Tehran has repeatedly promised to cooperate with the IAEA to defuse the situation and to halt the momentum for imposing further sanctions. Then, after the crisis is averted, it reneges on its promises and stonewalls IAEA requests for more information. These delaying tactics consume valuable time, which Iran has used to press ahead with its nuclear weapons research.

Unknowns About Iran's Nuclear Program

Many important things about Iran's nuclear program are simply not known because of Iran's systematic efforts to conceal and lie about its activities.

Unknown #1: How close is Iran to attaining a nuclear weapon?

It is not known when Iran will take the final steps to build a nuclear weapon. The uranium enrichment facility at Natanz is producing LEU at a rate that will give Tehran enough LEU by the end of July to build one nuclear device if the LEU is enriched further to weapons-grade levels. Tehran could then finish the enrichment process and amass enough highly punched uranium for a nuclear weapon by the end of the year [2010]. Natanz subsequently could produce enough LEU to permit construction of two bombs per year. Iran is also constructing a research reactor at Arak, which could begin producing weapons-grade plutonium as early as 2013.

Vice President Ali Akbar Salehi, the head of Iran's nuclear program, said on December 18 [2009] that Iran has been testing more advanced centrifuge models that will be installed in early 2011. These new models will be faster and more efficient than the old centrifuges, allowing Iran to accelerate the pace of its nuclear program. Salehi claimed that more than 6,000 centrifuges were enriching uranium, which is 2,000 more than the IAEA's November report indicated.

Some, including the U.S. intelligence community, believe that the Iranian leadership has not yet made the strategic decision to pursue nuclear weapons. This position has always been controversial given Iran's huge economic investment in the nuclear program, long-standing willingness to defy sanctions, and well-established pattern of confrontational behavior. It is now nearly impossible to defend this proposition after press reports of Iranian work on neutron initiators, the revelation of the clandestine Qom enrichment facility, and the IAEA's recent finding that Iran was working on a nuclear warhead for a missile.

Iran has relentlessly made steady progress on its nuclear weapons program and soon could acquire nuclear weapons.

Unknown #2: How extensive is Iranian–North Korean nuclear cooperation?

North Korea and Iran share a common hostility to the United States and have a long history of military and economic cooperation. Iran's ballistic missile force, the largest in the Middle East, is largely based on transferred North Korean missiles and weapon designs. North Korea has also sold Iran conventional weapons, including rocket launchers, small arms, and mini-submarines. The two countries are known to have close intelligence ties and to exchange intelligence regularly.

The extent of North Korean cooperation with Iran on nuclear issues remains unknown. However, both are known to have received help from A. Q. Khan's proliferation network. Iran helped to finance North Korea's nuclear program in exchange for nuclear technology and equipment, according to CIA [Central Intelligence Agency] sources cited in a 1993 *Economist Foreign Report*. Increased visits to Iran by North Korean nuclear specialists in 2003 reportedly led to a North Korea–Iran agreement for North Korea either to initiate or to accelerate work with Iranians to develop nuclear warheads that could be fitted on the North Korean No-Dong missiles, which North Korea and Iran were developing jointly. . . .

A Lack of Trustworthiness

Iran has relentlessly made steady progress on its nuclear weapons program and soon could acquire nuclear weapons. It continues to violate its IAEA safeguards agreement, refuses to comply with five U.N. Security Council resolutions on the nuclear issue, and has repeatedly been caught red-handed building secret nuclear facilities and violating U.N. Security Council resolutions that prohibit supplying arms to Hezbollah, its terrorist client group in Lebanon. Meanwhile, it has periodically tested missiles to trumpet its defiance, while systematically repressing and intimidating its own people after they objected to the fraudulent presidential elections in June.

On November 27, 2009, the IAEA Board of Governors passed a resolution demanding that Iran stop construction of the newly exposed uranium enrichment facility near Qom and referred the issue to the U.N. Security Council. This paves the way for expanded U.N. sanctions. Iran responded not only by refusing to halt enrichment efforts, but also by proclaiming its intention to undertake a massive expansion of its enrichment facilities. President Ahmadinejad unveiled plans to build 10 more enrichment plants at a cabinet meeting on November 29. Ali Larijani, the speaker of Iran's parliament who formerly led Iran's nuclear negotiations, warned that Iran may decide to withdraw from the Nuclear Non-Proliferation Treaty [Treaty on the Non-Proliferation of Nuclear Weapons].

Iran has consistently concealed and lied about its nuclear program and cannot be trusted to abide by any agreements it signs. British Foreign Secretary David Miliband complained that "Instead of engaging with us, Iran chooses to provoke and dissemble." On December 14, 2009, Secretary of State Hillary Clinton remarked:

> We have reached out. We have offered the opportunity to engage in meaningful, serious discussions with our Iranian counterparts. We have joined fully in the P−5+1 process. We've been at the table. But I don't think anyone can doubt that our outreach has produced very little in terms of any kind of positive response from the Iranians.

Ahmadinejad's regime has made a mockery of the Obama administration's engagement policy, which was based on the assumption that Iran's ruthless regime sought better relations with the United States and the West. Yet Iran's rulers fear Washington's friendship more than they fear its enmity. Their power and legitimacy is based on resistance to the United States ("the Great Satan") and enforcing Ayatollah Khamenei's harsh vision of God's will, not carrying out the will of their own people.

Iran is the world's foremost sponsor of terrorism and cannot be allowed to obtain the ultimate terrorist weapon: an atomic bomb.

The Obama administration's nuclear engagement strategy was also based on the assumption that Iran's unscrupulous Islamist regime could be trusted to come clean on the nuclear issue. This expectation was shattered on September 25, 2009, when President Obama announced in a joint press conference with British and French leaders that Western intelligence agencies had discovered another secret Iranian nuclear facility hidden inside a mountain near Qom. . . .

Iran is the world's foremost sponsor of terrorism and cannot be allowed to obtain the ultimate terrorist weapon: an atomic bomb. Yet Ahmadinejad's nuclear train rumbles onward. Unless the Obama administration alters its Iran strategy and moves rapidly to mobilize support for effective sanctions, there will eventually be a nuclear train wreck.

Yemen Is a Breeding Ground for Terrorists and a Threat to National Security

Christopher Boucek

Christopher Boucek is an associate in the Carnegie Endowment for International Peace Middle East program, where his research focuses on security challenges in the Persian Gulf and northern Africa.

With explosive devices sent to the United States from Yemen, attention is turning again to this country on the brink of total collapse—as it has in similar circumstances more than half a dozen times this year [2010] alone. Authorities are reportedly focusing on Yemen-based al Qaeda in the Arabian Peninsula (AQAP) as the source and possible mastermind behind a plot to bomb U.S. interests. In fact, security officials have had their eye on Yemen for some time as the country's instability and under-governed spaces provide a nearly perfect haven for terrorists. AQAP is now a bigger risk to U.S. national security than al Qaeda's central leaders hiding in South Asia.

Al Qaeda in Yemen

Yemen has been on everyone's map since last year's failed Christmas Day attack on a flight headed for Detroit. And attention has continued with the notoriety of U.S.-born cleric Anwar al-Awlaki, who calls for deadly strikes on the United States from his place of refuge in Yemen. The attention and support Yemen garners, however, pales in comparison to al Qaeda central in South Asia.

But the threat coming out of other states of concern—not only Pakistan and Afghanistan, but also Somalia—is not as immediate as the danger from Yemen and AQAP. While al Qaeda central has been under continuous danger with an aggressive drone campaign in Pakistan and a large U.S. military presence in Afghanistan, AQAP is relatively free to operate within Yemen's borders.

AQAP was officially announced in January 2009 following the merger of the militant outfits in Saudi Arabia and Yemen. While it modeled itself on the original group, it is autonomous and doesn't take direction from Osama bin Laden. AQAP is agile, opportunistic, and, most dangerously, they learn from their mistakes and try again.

Despite Western security assistance and the clandestine use of U.S. air strikes, al Qaeda is surging in Yemen and the pace of its attacks is intensifying. Within the country, there have already been more than forty attacks this year and around sixty Yemeni security officials have been killed in the violence.

Problems in a Failing State

Yemen has a long history of terrorism and extremism and is strategically located between Saudi Arabia and Somalia—serving as a bridge between the Arabian Peninsula and the Horn of Africa. There were many Yemenis who fought in Afghanistan in the 1980s against the Soviet occupation and there was a large contingent of Yemenis in al Qaeda training camps before 9/11 [September 11, 2001, terrorist attacks on the United States]. Additionally, al Qaeda's very first attack on an American target took place in Yemen two decades ago, and this year marked the tenth anniversary of the USS *Cole* bombing on Yemen's coast that killed seventeen U.S. sailors.

Besides the resurgent al Qaeda organization, the country faces an ongoing civil war in the north, an increasingly violent secessionist movement in the south, inadequate governance, economic ruin and is quickly running out of water. And while many failing states confront similar problems, Yemen is unique in that it is dealing with them all at the same time. In fact, these are the real dangers facing Yemen—even more so than terrorism.

With an expanding recruiting pool of increasingly poor, undereducated and underemployed men, AQAP has firmly taken root in Yemen, capitalizing on the absence of the central government and widespread poverty and instability to spread their message. And the group's ability to frame the situation in Yemen and cast U.S. military assistance and counterterrorism strikes as an American occupation has drawn foreign terrorists to the country. Yemen is now an inspiration to foreign-based extremists.

The Need to Focus on Yemen

While the details of this latest incident are still being revealed, it's clear that the U.S. national security threat emanating from Yemen continues to rise. With a balanced approach, Washington can limit al Qaeda's reach out of Yemen. The solution is not found in an exclusive reliance on counterterrorism and military assistance, but in a greater concentration on helping Yemen confront the converging challenges. A singular focus on counterterrorism will only increase the danger for America.

With this in mind, Washington must find a way to help Yemeni leaders improve government and social services, fight corruption, encourage economic development and deal with the legitimate grievances of resistance groups. Long-term development and financial assistance is one of the best ways to do this, but Washington devotes a disproportionately small sum today. This is clear when looking at the resources devoted to Yemen and Pakistan—they don't match the relative dangers. The United States intends to send almost $200 million to Yemen, but Pakistan expects to receive billions next year.

If President [Barack] Obama is serious in helping to build a "stable, secure, and prosperous" Yemen, as he said Friday

shortly after the bombs were discovered, then he should ap-
point a special representative to globally coordinate U.S. policy
on Yemen. This needs to be someone with the gravitas to or-
ganize disparate international aid efforts and push the Yemeni
government to address their systemic challenges. The country's
problems are too important to ignore—this latest incident
only underscores that Yemen's problems are America's problems too.

Given the risk terrorists in the country pose, the United
States must remain focused on all of the problems facing Yemen—only then can the nearly flawless setting for terrorist
activity be contained.

CHAPTER 2

How Can the Israeli-Palestinian Conflict Be Resolved?

Overview: Resolving the Israeli-Palestinian Conflict

Jim Zanotti

Jim Zanotti is an analyst in Middle Eastern Affairs for the Congressional Research Service, a legislative branch government agency that provides policy and legal analysis to committees and members of Congress regardless of party affiliation.

It has now been 16 years since Israel and the PLO [Palestine Liberation Organization] agreed to the 1993 Oslo Accord [a peace agreement between the Israeli government and Palestinians]. Yet, differences between the sides over core issues, such as borders, security, settlements, the status of Jerusalem, refugees, and water rights, have not been overcome, despite the third-party involvement of various international actors—the United States, in particular.

A Two-State Solution

Previously when talks have faltered, the parties eventually returned to the negotiating table, and some observers are convinced that this option is likely to remain viable so long as it is supported politically. Yet there are a number of key actors and observers expressing doubts that the very concept of a negotiated two-state solution can survive a process in which negotiations are put on hold and resumed an indefinite number of times without finality. These doubts have been exacerbated by geopolitical changes and by realities on the ground—including demographics, violence, Palestinian factionalism, Israeli settlements, and other impediments to Palestinian movement and territorial contiguity—that sustain tensions between Israelis and Palestinians. The Israeli daily *Ha'aretz* reported a

Jim Zanotti, "Israel and the Palestinians: Prospects for a Two-State Solution," Congressional Research Service, January 8, 2010, pp. 2–3, 11–12, 24. Opencrs.com.

"senior U.S. administration" source's account of what President [Barack] Obama told [Israeli Prime Minister Benjamin] Netanyahu and [chairman of the PLO Mahmoud] Abbas during the closed-door session of the September 2009 trilateral meeting in New York: "We've had enough talks. We need to end this conflict. There is a window of opportunity but it might shut."

Decreased hope in the viability of a two-state solution has led to a willingness among some policy makers and analysts to consider different pathways to get there—such as Palestinian statehood prior to a final-status agreement or a "borders first" deal. It also has led to openness among some Israelis and Palestinians to alternative solutions that are contrary to declared U.S. policy. These alternatives, each of which is the subject of considerable debate among and between Israelis and Palestinians, include a so-called "one-state solution," a "Jordanian" or "regional" option, or other, non-negotiated outcomes. Continued failure to reach a two-state solution, combined with lack of consensus on any of the alternatives, may also mean that the status quo in the West Bank and Gaza could continue indefinitely. Polls indicate that significant majorities in various Arab states believe that a collapse in prospects for a two-state solution could lead to a "state of intense conflict for years to come." . . .

Alternatives to a Two-State Solution

Proponents of the two-state idea might argue that it would be better to strengthen existing political will for a two-state solution than to spend time and resources building a new consensus for one or more alternative solutions. A quest for alternatives might more accurately reflect a "grass is always greener" mentality than a qualitatively superior approach to resolving the conflict. On the other hand, opponents of the two-state idea might argue that recycling a framework that has fallen short for over a decade and a half is unwise and that something new should be tried instead of sinking more political capital into what could be an irredeemably failed idea.

In an August 2009 *New York Times* column, former U.S. Special Assistant to the President for Arab-Israeli Affairs (under President [Bill] Clinton) Robert Malley—now the director of the Middle East program at the International Crisis Group—and Hussein Agha argued that rhetorical support for a two-state solution by Benjamin Netanyahu and Khaled Meshaal [a leader of Hamas, a Palestinian Islamic political party] with all their caveats and qualifications, may be more a sign that the term "two-state solution" has been drained of its explanatory value than that a peaceful resolution is any closer:

> This nearly unanimous consensus is the surest sign to date that the two-state solution has become void of meaning, a catchphrase divorced from the contentious issues it is supposed to resolve. Everyone can say yes because saying yes no longer says much, and saying no has become too costly. Acceptance of the two-state solution signals continuation of the Israeli-Palestinian struggle by other means. . . .

Lack of Israeli-Palestinian consensus on any of these alternatives may mean that the status quo in the West Bank and Gaza could continue.

In the same column, Malley and Agha postulated that past attempts to resolve the conflict might have paid too little attention to the questions of identity and narrative that fuel Israeli-Palestinian disagreement on issues such as permanent security arrangements, the status of Jerusalem, Palestinian refugees, and the settlements.

> That so many attempts to resolve the conflict have failed is reason to be wary. . . . It is hard today to imagine a resolution that does not entail two states. But two states may not be a true resolution if the roots of this clash are ignored.

The ultimate territorial outcome almost certainly will be found within the borders of 1967. To be sustainable, it will need to grapple with matters left over since 1948. . . .

In the closed-door session of the September 2009 trilateral meeting in New York, President Obama reportedly laid out the following vision for negotiations to Netanyahu and Abbas:

There's an historical record of the entire past negotiations and there are principles. We won't start the negotiations from scratch, we will not take the historical record and toss it aside. Nor will we wait for the perfect formula. . . . It's difficult to disentangle ourselves from history but we must do so. The only reason to hold public office is to get things done. We all must take risks for peace.

The Risks of the Status Quo

How the logistics of a land-for-peace compromise might be resolved at the same time the conflicting worldviews of Israelis and Palestinians are addressed or transcended remains unclear. Also unclear is whether calls for new ways to conceptualize and/or resolve the conflict might increase in frequency and intensity—compelling the Israelis, Palestinians, United States, and/or other international actors to respond—if future proposals advanced under the "two-state solution" heading are perceived to stretch the reasonable elasticity of the term to its breaking point. . . .

As warnings have grown more frequent and emphatic that the window of opportunity for a two-state solution might be closing, several proposals for other ways to address the future of the Palestinian territories have surfaced from both the Palestinian and the Israeli sides. Some of these proposals are not altogether new, but rather existed in some form before a two-state solution became the official Israeli and PLO line. Some analysts suggest that raising alternatives is a time-honored tactic employed to jump-start or to galvanize negotiations. Others perceive that the advent of alternative proposals reflects a shift in fundamental realities underlying the public discourse on the peace process that makes a two-state solution less likely as time passes. Lack of Israeli-Palestinian consensus on any of these alternatives may mean that the status quo in the West Bank and Gaza could continue.

A Two-State Solution Is Possible for Israelis and Palestinians

John V. Whitbeck

John V. Whitbeck is an international lawyer who has advised the Palestinian negotiation team in talks with Israel.

As the Israeli-Palestinian "peace process" struggles to inch forward again in an atmosphere of profound pessimism bordering on hopelessness, what is most sadly missing is any compelling vision of how a Holy Land at peace could be structured so as to enhance not only the physical security of Israelis and the human dignity of Palestinians but also the future quality of day-to-day life for both peoples.

The Declaration of Principles so optimistically signed on the White House lawn in September 1993 proclaimed as its goal a "historic reconciliation" between the two peoples. Today, even optimists seem to hope only for a definitive separation of the two peoples behind high walls and fences.

A Two-State Solution

Can Israelis and Palestinians really do no better than this? Might it not still be possible to blend the practical and psychological preferences of both peoples for a two-state solution with some of the best aspects of a humane one-state solution to produce a vision of a possible future so bright and appealing that both Israelis and Palestinians would be inspired to act on their hopes and dreams, rather than their memories and fears, and to seize this future together and make it a reality?

Sharing the Holy Land is not a zero-sum game in which any development advantageous to one side must be disadvan-

John V. Whitbeck, "Two States, One Holy Land: A Framework for Peace," *Washington Report on Middle East Affairs*, November 2010, pp. 22–23. www.wrmea.com. Copyright © 2010 by American Educational Trust. All rights reserved. Reproduced by permission.

tageous to the other. One can envisage a society in which, by separating political and voting rights from economic, social and residential rights in a negotiated settlement, both the legitimate national aspirations of Palestinians and the legitimate security interests of Israelis could be simultaneously satisfied.

The Holy Land could be a two-state "confederation," a single economic and social unit encompassing two sovereign states and one Holy City. Jerusalem could be an Israeli-Palestinian "condominium," an open city forming an undivided part of both states, being the capital of both states and being administered by local district councils and an umbrella municipal council.

All current residents of the Holy Land could be given the choice of Israeli or Palestinian citizenship, thus determining which state's passport they would carry and in which state's national elections they would vote. All citizens of either state could vote in municipal elections where they actually live—a matter of particular relevance to current Palestinian citizens of Israel opting for Palestinian citizenship and to Israeli settlers choosing to continue to live in Palestine while maintaining their Israeli citizenship. Each state could have its own "law of return" conferring citizenship and residential rights within that state on persons not currently resident in the Holy Land.

Borders would have to be drawn on maps but would not have to exist on the ground. The free, nondiscriminatory movement of people and goods within the Holy Land could be a fundamental principle subject only to one major exception: to ensure that each state would always maintain its national character, the right to residence in each Holy Land state could be limited to that state's citizens, to citizens of the other state residing there on an agreed date, and to their descendants. (In this way, deeply felt principles could be maintained. Israelis could have the right to live in all of Eretz Israel—but not all Israelis in all of Eretz Israel. Similarly, Palestinians could have the right to live in all of historical Palestine—but not all Palestinians in all of historical Palestine.) A common currency (perhaps printed in Hebrew on one side and Arabic on the other) could be issued by a common central bank.

To ease Israeli security concerns, the Palestinian state could be fully demilitarized, with no one other than Palestinian police allowed to bear arms within its territory. As an essential counterpart to the absence of border controls within the Holy Land, Israel could conduct immigration controls for entry into Israel, at the same time that Palestine conducts immigration controls for entry into Palestine, at the frontiers of the Palestinian state with Egypt and Jordan, with any non-Palestinian visitors restricted to the Palestinian state by the Israeli authorities facing penalties if found in Israel. The settlement agreement could be guaranteed by the United Nations [U.N.] and relevant states, with international tribunals to arbitrate disputes regarding compliance with its terms.

A Shared Jerusalem

The status of Jerusalem poses the toughest problem for any settlement plan—causing many to assume, for this reason alone, that no settlement acceptable to both sides can ever be reached. When the U.N. General Assembly adopted Resolution 181 in 1947, it addressed the problem by suggesting an international status for Jerusalem, with neither the Jewish state nor the Arab state to have sovereignty over the city. Yet joint undivided sovereignty, while rare, is not without precedent.

Chandigarh is the joint undivided capital of two Indian states. For half a century, Sudan was a condominium of Britain and Egypt, officially named "Anglo-Egyptian Sudan." For more than 70 years, the Pacific Islands state of Vanuatu (formerly the New Hebrides Condominium) was under the joint undivided sovereignty of Britain and France. For more than 700 years, until a 1993 constitutional revision, the Principality of Andorra was under the joint undivided sovereignty of French and Spanish "co-princes." In March 1999, the arbitrator appointed by the International Court of Justice ruled that the contested Bosnian municipality of Brcko should be a condominium shared by Bosnia's Serb Republic and its Muslim-Croat Federation.

Jerusalem could be a symbol of reconciliation and hope for Jews, Muslims, Christians and the world as a whole.

As a joint capital, Jerusalem could have Israeli government offices principally in its western sector, Palestinian government offices principally in its eastern sector, and municipal offices in both. A system of districts or French-style *arrondissements* could bring municipal government closer to the different communities in the city (including the ultra-Orthodox Jewish community), with local district councils dealing with all matters best dealt with locally and an umbrella municipal council dealing only with those matters requiring citywide coordination. To the extent that either state wished to control people or goods passing into it from the other state, this could be done at the points of exit from, rather than the points of entry to, Jerusalem. In a context of peace, particularly one coupled with economic union, the need for such controls would be minimal.

In a sense, Jerusalem can be viewed as a cake which could be sliced either vertically or horizontally. Either way, both Israelis and Palestinians would get a share of the cake, but, while many Israelis could never voluntarily swallow a vertical slice, they might just be able to swallow a horizontal slice. Indeed, by doing so, Israel would finally achieve international recognition of Jerusalem as its capital. Embassies to Israel, all of which are currently located in Tel Aviv in a reflection of the nonrecognition by the international community of Israel's claim to sovereignty over Jerusalem, could be expected to move there.

Jerusalem is both a municipality on the ground and a symbol in hearts and minds. Undivided but shared in this way, Jerusalem could be a symbol of reconciliation and hope for Jews, Muslims, Christians and the world as a whole. It would be so even if the "condominium" principle of joint undivided sovereignty were formally applied only to the contested heart of Jerusalem, notably the Old City and the Mount of Olives, with sovereignty over the other parts of an open city being assigned to one or the other of the two states.

The Advantages for Both Sides

Such a framework would address in ways advantageous to both sides three of the principal practical problems on the road to peace: Jerusalem (through joint sovereignty over an undivided city), settlers (through a separation of citizenship rights from residential rights in a regime of free access to the entire Holy Land for all citizens of both states under which no one would be compelled to move), and borders (through a structure of relations between the two states so open and non-threatening that the precise placement of borders would no longer be such a contentious issue and the internationally recognized pre-1967 borders—subject only to the expanded borders of Jerusalem, under joint sovereignty—might well be acceptable to most Israelis, as they would certainly be to most Palestinians).

For Jewish Israelis, the rapidly approaching inevitability of living in a state with either a majority of Arab voters or an inescapable resemblance to pre-1990 South Africa and worldwide pariah status would be replaced by the assurance of living in a democratic state with fewer Arab voters than today. Israel's security would be enhanced by assuaging, rather than continuing to aggravate, the Palestinians' grievances and the hatred throughout the Arab and Muslim worlds based upon the perpetuation of those grievances. By escaping from the role (so tragic in light of Jewish history) of oppressors and enforcers of injustice, Israel would save its soul and its dreams.

For all Palestinians, human dignity would be restored. They would cease to be a people treated (and not only by Israelis) as uniquely unworthy of basic human rights. For those in exile, an internationally accepted Palestinian citizenship, a Palestinian passport and a right to return to all of pre-1948 Palestine, if only to visit, would have enormous significance.

Furthermore, if the Palestinians themselves accepted a settlement, all Arab states would establish normal diplomatic and commercial relations with Israel, as has been made clear in the Arab Peace Initiative of 2002, which remains on the table, waiting to be seized by Israel. If a Palestinian flag were peacefully raised over Palestinian government offices in Jerusalem, few Arab or Muslim eyes would still see Israel through a veil of hatred. The immovable obstacle to a lasting region-wide peace would have been removed.

Israelis, Palestinians and the true friends of both must now resist the temptation to despair, raise their sights and pursue a compelling vision of a society so much better than the status quo.

The Requirements for Acceptance

While implementation of such a framework for peace would be relatively simple (far more so than traditional "two-state solutions" premised on the separation of Israelis and Palestinians), its acceptance would require a moral, spiritual and psychological transformation from both Israelis and Palestinians. Yet, given the decades of hatred, bitterness and distrust, aggravated by the past 17 years of a failed and seemingly perpetual "peace process," any settlement would require such a transformation.

Precisely because such a transformation would be so difficult, it is far more likely to be achieved if both peoples can be inspired by a truly compelling vision of a new society of peaceful coexistence, mutual respect and human dignity, in which both peoples are winners, than if they are left to contemplate painful programs for a new partition and an angry separation in which both peoples must regard themselves, to a considerable degree, as admitting defeat.

Israelis, Palestinians and the true friends of both must now resist the temptation to despair, raise their sights and pursue a compelling vision of a society so much better than the status quo that both Israelis and Palestinians are inspired to accept in their hearts and minds that peace is both desirable and attainable, that the Holy Land can be shared, that a winner-take-all approach produces only losers, that both Israelis and Palestinians must be winners or both will continue to be losers, and that there is a common destination at which both peoples would be satisfied to arrive and to live together.

Support for a One-State Solution for Israelis and Palestinians Is Increasing

Danny Rubinstein

Danny Rubinstein is a specialist on Arab and Palestinian affairs who teaches at Ben-Gurion University of the Negev and the Hebrew University of Jerusalem.

Against the background of Barack Obama's attempt to defend the idea of "two states for two peoples" in Israel/ Palestine, consider a recent talk given by the Palestinian Sufian Abu Zayda. Abu Zayda is fifty years old. He was born in the Jabalya refugee camp in northern Gaza, the largest of the Palestinian camps, and he is considered the Palestinian spokesman most fluent in Hebrew, which he learned during the fourteen years that he spent in an Israeli prison on charges of participating in terrorist activities. After his release in 1993, he was one of the senior Fatah leaders in Gaza and was appointed to various positions in the Palestinian government. Among other activities he has been active in the Israeli-Palestinian Geneva Initiative, in which moderates from both sides argue that it is possible to find a just two-state solution.

Israeli Support for a Palestinian State

It was quite surprising, therefore, that Abu Zayda, in his talk to an Israeli audience, announced that he had changed his mind. Like other Palestinians who spoke to the Israeli media over the last months, he was responding to Prime Minister Benjamin Netanyahu's speech at Bar-Ilan University—itself a response of sorts to President [Barack] Obama's June 2009 speech at the University of Cairo. With some drama, Netanyahu had agreed that a Palestinian state should be established in territory of the Land of Israel to the west of the Jordan River. This was a significant change for Netanyahu, whose roots are in the nationalist movement that has given up its earlier slogan—"There are two banks to the Jordan, this one is ours, and so is that one"—but that still demands Israeli rule in the "Greater" Land of Israel west of the Jordan. Commentators talked of a "fissure" on the Israeli Right; it was widely believed that as long as Ben Zion Netanyahu is still alive, his son wouldn't dare rebel against the nationalist traditions of the family.

But what might have seemed unbelievable a short time ago has become a reality. Netanyahu, at the head of the nationalist, right-wing government with members like Benny Begin (son of Menachem Begin) who have consistently rejected all concessions, has accepted the idea of a Palestinian state.

On both sides, the accepted assumption is that although everyone wants a two-state solution, the actual situation is pushing everyone toward a one-state solution.

In his talk at Tel Aviv University, Abu Zayda responded to what the prime minister had said: "Many thanks to Benjamin Netanyahu. After twenty years of the peace process [since the Madrid Conference in 1991], and after the mutual recognition of Israel and the PLO [Palestine Liberation Organization] [in the Oslo Accords], he finally agrees to a Palestinian state." There was irony in his voice as he continued, "Do you think you are doing us a favor when you agree to two states? No favor at all. From my side, from the Palestinians' side—let there be one state, not two. . . . I was introduced to you as Sufian Abu Zayda from the Jabalya camp, but I'm not from Jabalya. I might have been born there, but my family had been exiled in 1948 from a village named 'Breer,' where kibbutz Bror Hayil now stands, near the Gaza border. If there will be one state, I'll be happy to rent or buy a house near the kibbutz and live there." And then Abu Zayda said in a loud voice, "You are doing yourselves a favor by establishing two states, not us."

He isn't alone in his opinion. One can sense a great change among Palestinians—a new lack of trust in the possibility of a Palestinian state. In Ramallah, Nablus, and Hebron, people are talking and writing about this. It is interesting that the shift is taking place at the very time when the whole world is united in pressing Israel to help the Palestinians create a state of their own. The Obama administration, the European Union, Russia, those Arab states that still maintain their initiative of almost a decade ago (to establish peace with Israel in exchange for its withdrawal to the 1967 border)—all of them seek a two-state solution. Even Netanyahu's Israel is ready for it. So who thinks that it's no longer a useful idea? The Palestinians—but not all of them, of course. . . .

The Palestinian Nationalist Movement

On both sides, the accepted assumption is that although everyone wants a two-state solution, the actual situation is pushing everyone toward a one-state solution. This is a solution that no one wants, but that's what is happening. In the background is the most important political development of the past few years—the decline of the Palestinian nationalist movement.

From its beginnings at the start of the twentieth century, the Palestinian movement has had one clear goal: to free itself from foreign occupation, first from the British and then from the Israelis. The demand to create a Palestinian state does not appear in the national covenant that the PLO proclaimed in the 1960s. And in the short period in which most Palestinians lived under Arab rule (from 1948 to 1967), they did not work for the establishment of a state in the West Bank and Gaza.

It was after the 1967 war that the demand for a state was formulated and the Palestinian national movement reached its peak strength. [Palestinian leader] Yasser Arafat and his comrades from the Fatah movement took over the PLO, which had been founded by the attorney Ahmad Shuqayri with the support of Egyptian president Gamal Abdel Nasser. In Arafat's renewed PLO, all the ideological tendencies found a home: nationalists, religious believers, socialists, Marxists, Communists, Pan-Arabists, and conservatives—as well as groups operating under the sponsorship of the "revolutionary" regimes of Syria and Iraq. There were even groups sponsored by King Hussein of Jordan, who was suspicious of all Palestinian nationalists and who in the end fought against them in the "Black September" of 1970, which ended with the flight of the PLO leadership to Beirut. Even from there, it continued to shape the Palestinian struggle as a unified national cause.

Those glory days are long gone. Since the failure of the Oslo Accords and the outbreak of the bloody clashes in 2000 (the "al-Aqsa Intifada"), the Palestinian public has been split and fragmented—and so has the PLO. In Gaza, Hamas, a movement tied to the Muslim Brotherhood, rules. Throughout its history, the Brotherhood has made nationalism secondary to Islamic religious identity. Hamas was never part of the PLO, and it does not see itself obligated to keep agreements with Israel or to subscribe to the ideology of Palestinian nationalism. Because of the failure of the PLO and Fatah to create a Palestinian state and because of the widespread sense that their leadership is corrupt, Hamas has gained strength on the West Bank.

In the past, thousands of young Arab citizens of Israel supported the PLO. One example is the poet Mahmoud Darwish, who left Israel to work with the PLO. But for the past few years the aspiration of many has been in the opposite direction. Some Palestinians who defined themselves as PLO loyalists have returned, or asked to return, and become regular

Israeli citizens. One of them, Sabri Jiryis, editor of Palestinian journals and the head of the PLO archive, has come back to his birthplace, the village of Fasuta in the Galilee. After the Palestinian Authority was established in 1994, researchers asked Israeli Arabs if they would like to live under Palestinian national rule. Those polled lived in "the triangle," the Arab areas of Israel closest to the West Bank border. The response of the majority of those polled (approximately 80 percent) was always negative. In the past few years, this majority has grown. In one of the last polls, 96 percent of the villagers of Wadi Ara said that they were not willing to accept any arrangement in which the Palestinian Authority would rule their area.

The city won't be divided, and so they are adapting to a situation that will lead in the end to a single state.

Palestinian Requests for Israeli Citizenship

Extraordinary things are now happening, without much publicity, in another Palestinian community, that of the 300,000 Arabs of East Jerusalem. In the past few years, tens of thousands of them have applied to the Ministry of the Interior for full Israeli citizenship. In 1967, when East Jerusalem was annexed to Israel, its inhabitants were given "temporary resident" status, not citizenship. This resembles the U.S. green card, except that it does not serve as a way station to full citizenship. Temporary residents have all the rights and obligations of a regular citizen—they pay taxes and receive the benefits of the social welfare system. But they cannot vote in parliamentary elections or carry an Israeli passport.

That they can't vote for Knesset [Israel's legislature] members has not bothered the Jerusalem Arabs, nor has the lack of a passport—the government gives travelers an Israeli "Laisser-Passer." The problem, from their vantage point, is that they can lose their temporary resident status if they don't continue to live in Jerusalem. Indeed, the Interior Ministry has taken away temporary resident cards from thousands of Jerusalem Arabs who moved to areas in the West Bank or who have lived overseas for a few years.

Hence the growing number of requests for full Israeli citizenship. There are many difficulties in the way. The most serious is that such a request is considered as collaboration with the enemy, the conqueror, and therefore a betrayal of Palestinian nationalism. That's why so few applied in the years after the 1967 war—and most of them were Jerusalem Arabs who married Israeli Arabs. The PLO and the Palestinian Authority government in Ramallah have decided to fight the new trend. They sent representatives to the East Jerusalem office of the Interior Ministry and warned those standing on line not to request the citizenship application forms.

Despite the warnings, the number of applicants is growing. A spokesman for the ministry told me that in the last two years, about twelve thousand Palestinians from East Jerusalem have received Israeli citizenship. What is most significant here is that there isn't any embarrassment about applying for it. A Palestinian journalist told me, "Not only are they not embarrassed, they are proud that they have succeeded in getting Israeli citizenship." This is the strongest possible example of the low point that Palestinian nationalism has reached—at least in the eyes of the Palestinians of Jerusalem. They now believe that the Israeli (Jewish) presence in the eastern part of the city is so powerful that it cannot be shaken or dislodged. The city won't be divided, and so they are adapting to a situation that will lead in the end to a single state.

The Decline of the PLO

The decline of the Palestinian national movement can be seen in even sharper relief in the center of its power on the West Bank. Since its founding in 1964, the PLO's three leading bodies have been the National Council, the Central Council, and the Executive Committee. Representation in those bodies was apportioned among the various Palestinian organizations that existed fifty years ago. This proportional representation remains as it was, and it has turned the PLO into an outdated, pathetic, useless institution that barely functions. Its whole purpose is to provide meager salaries to its functionaries. In its councils and committees, Marxist groups like the Popular Front for the Liberation of Palestine, which has split into factions over the years, are still represented, as are the Democratic Front, the Communist Party, and other ephemeral organizations whose existence has been forgotten and who have almost no public support.

By contrast, the PLO has no representatives of Hamas and Islamic Jihad, two movements that together probably have the support of more than a third of the Palestinian public.

Abu Mazen [also known as Mahmoud Abbas] continues to convene the councils of the PLO, but it is hard to find people who take seriously their deliberations and decisions. The Israeli and Arab media report every utterance made by the leaders of Hamas, but pay much less attention to the pronouncements of PLO spokesmen.

The new Palestinian generation in the West Bank (less so in Gaza), who know Israel so well, would prefer to fight for equal rights in a single binational state.

Similar observations could be made about the decline of the Fatah movement, the ruling party in the PLO and the Palestinian Authority. Fatah was weakened when some of its leaders, like Farouk Kaddoumi, objected to the Oslo Accords and refused to live under the Palestinian autonomy, the "state-in-the-making" that was established in the West Bank and Gaza. When he died in 2004, Arafat left behind a movement that was also dying and a leadership widely thought to be corrupt. At the head of the Fatah movement is the Central Committee, a group of eighteen people whose power resembles that of the Politburo in Communist regimes. Only fourteen members were still alive, all over seventy, in August 2009, when a new committee was finally elected. . . .

The Newly Elected Younger Guard

In Bethlehem, in August of 2009, the Fatah general assembly met for the first time in almost twenty years. At this meeting, new leaders were elected. For the Central Committee positions there were twenty-two candidates, fourteen of whom were new figures in the movement. Left on the committee were some of the old-timers, members of Abu Mazen's faction. But the main change was in the profile of the younger elected members (Khalil Shikaki, the sociologist and researcher from Ramallah, calls them the "young guard," but the truth is that most of them are over fifty).

Prominent among them are Marwan Barghouti, now imprisoned in Israel after being convicted of organizing terror attacks; Jibril Rajoub and Muhammad Dahlan, the two heads of the Palestinian Security Services, who spent many years in Israeli jails; and other activists, such as Muhammad Shatiyah, Hussein al-Shaykh, and Muhammad al-Madani. These younger men were born, grew up, and came to maturity in the Palestinian territories of the West Bank and Gaza under Israeli rule. Their background is totally different from those of Abu Mazen and his generation, the Fatah veterans. The veterans grew up in refugee camps in Jordan, Syria, and Lebanon, or they left the camps of Gaza when they were still children. They studied in the universities of Cairo, Damascus, and Beirut—and traveled on Fatah business all over the world. Most of them have a revolutionary and secular orientation, the result of the support that the Palestinian movement once received from the Communist bloc. When they arrived with Arafat at the West Bank and Gaza, they were seen as somewhat "foreign." The accusation was that they brought with them a culture that was not appropriate to the traditional culture of the territories—nightclubs, parties, large expenditures, and a luxurious lifestyle. These were the legacy of the years when the PLO was flush with funds—especially after [Egyptian president Anwar] Sadat's "peace initiative" of 1977, when the Arab states, especially Iraq, bought and paid for PLO resistance to the Egyptian initiative.

National unity has dissolved . . . and the idea has become acceptable that if there won't be two states for two peoples, it is better that there be one state.

After many years outside of Palestine, the older activists have a familiarity with, and an attachment to, the Arab world. They are at home in the countries in which they grew up, studied, and lived. This is not true of the recently elected younger guard. Their whole lives have been spent in the homeland, in the cities, villages, and refugee camps of the West Bank and Gaza. They know Tel Aviv and the Israeli reality far better than the reality of Damascus and Cairo. After years in Israeli prisons or at work in Israel, there are those among them who have total mastery of the Hebrew language. They are interviewed regularly in Hebrew in the Israeli media, and they participate in Israeli events. They have Israeli friends, both Jews and Arabs, and they visit these friends at home in West Jerusalem, Herzliya, Haifa, or Nazareth.

They have no family or property in Amman or Cairo, and thus they are more like the Palestinian citizens of Israel than they are like the members of the old guard. It would not be a great exaggeration to assert that the new Palestinian generation in the West Bank (less so in Gaza), who know Israel so well, would prefer to fight for equal rights in a single binational state rather than continue a struggle that seems almost hopeless—to establish an independent state.

A Decline in Nationalism

This is not a casual suggestion or a guess. In the past few years, Palestinian figures have talked about ending the discouraging struggle to create Palestinian rule in the territories. Sari Nusseibeh, president of Al-Quds University, once suggested, with a degree of cynicism, that the Palestinians should demand total annexation so that they could receive the same rights as Israelis in the common homeland. Ali Jarbawi of Birzeit University has raised the possibility of a voluntary dismantling of the Palestinian Authority.

In international diplomacy there is a pervasive idea that it is possible and necessary to establish a Palestinian state in the West Bank and Gaza that will exist side by side with Israel. Many Israelis and Palestinians want this and believe in it. But the forces working against this possibility are many and powerful. Israeli governments have enabled the settlement of over half a million Jews beyond the 1967 borders. This represents almost 10 percent of the Jews in Israel. About 300,000 of them live in settlements in the West Bank and about 200,000 are in the Jewish neighborhoods of East Jerusalem. There are those among them who will fight with all their strength to prevent an Israeli withdrawal and the establishment of a Palestinian state. But what is no less important is that on the Palestinian side as well a new situation has emerged. National unity has dissolved, the national movement has atrophied and declined, and the idea has become acceptable that if there won't be two states for two peoples, it is better that there be one state.

A Parallel State Structure Is the Solution for Israelis and Palestinians

Mathias Mossberg and Mark LeVine

Mathias Mossberg directs the Parallel States Project at the Center for Middle Eastern Studies at Lund University in Sweden. Mark LeVine is a professor of Middle Eastern History at the University of California, Irvine; a visiting senior researcher at Lund University; and the author of Impossible Peace: Israel/Palestine Since 1989.

Growing US-Israeli tension over continued East Jerusalem settlement construction—which the White House appears unable to stop—underscores a deeper reality: The two-state solution is no longer possible.

The Two-State Solution

The occupied territories are politically, economically, and geographically so deeply integrated into Israel that there is no practical way to transfer them to Palestinian sovereignty within the framework of a two-state solution.

Israeli scholars have been warning of this to anyone who would listen for over two decades.

While they cannot say so publicly, given the events that have transpired since Vice President [Joe] Biden's visit to Jerusalem in March [2010], President [Barack] Obama, Mr. Biden, Secretary of State [Hillary] Clinton and the rest of the Washington foreign-policy establishment may be slowly waking up to the reality that it is simply not possible to establish a viable Palestinian state in the occupied territories.

The question is: Does the US government have a "Plan B" for bringing peace to the Holy Land outside the moribund Oslo [Accords] framework?

With almost two decades invested in the Oslo process, the thought of its demise, and with it that of the two-state solution as currently envisioned, is disheartening and frightening. Yet Oslo was always an impossible peace, doomed to fail precisely because it was premised not merely on the notion of two antagonistic, exclusivist nationalist movements peacefully dividing a pint-sized territory, but on doing so while the balance of power—and thus the conflict's resolution—remained severely skewed toward the stronger side.

As long as the US won't force Israel to chose between the settlements in the West Bank and Jerusalem and unquestioning American support, Israel has no reason to make painful concessions to an ever-weaker Palestinian side.

The situation has come to a deadlock. It is time for a rethink.

As the two-state solution seems increasingly implausible, voices for a one-state or binational solution become stronger. But a one-state solution is equally unrealistic—the whole raison d'être for the state of Israel is to provide a Jewish state for the Jews. And there are no signs or prospects of change in this basic Israeli position as long as it holds most of the cards.

The Parallel State Alternative

For the past few years, we have been participating in numerous meetings with high-level Israeli and Palestinian policy makers, scholars, and commentators, discussing alternative scenarios, including one that we describe as a "parallel states" structure.

Essentially, the idea suggests the creation of two-state structures on the same land, both covering the whole territory, both providing the freedom for their citizens—Israelis and Palestinians—to live between the Mediterranean Sea and the Jordan River.

The most important innovation of a parallel state structure is that state sovereignty would be linked primarily with the individual citizen, and only in a secondary way with territory. Separating the territorial and citizenship/identity dimensions of sovereignty would allow Israelis and Palestinians to retain their national symbols, have political and legislative bodies that are responsible to their own electorate, and retain a high degree of political independence.

Precisely by no longer defining sovereignty through exclusive control over territory, this structure would enable the creation of an independent Palestinian state while preserving the state of Israel, both Jewish and democratic. The contours of political authority and security would be shared by the two states in a manner that guarantees the long-term secure existence of each community. It would be guaranteed by international treaty and, if necessary, a strong international monitoring presence.

Legal, educational, and other functions that pertain to each state's relationship with citizens would be exercised separately, while those that necessarily encompass the whole territory would be shared or in common.

A parallel state structure would allow Israelis and Palestinians to live anywhere in the territory of Israel/Palestine, yet retain citizenship in their ethnic homeland. Jews could live throughout their biblical heartland, the West Bank, while Palestinians could return in significant numbers to Israel without upsetting the demographic balance that guarantees Jewish control of the Israeli state.

Bringing an end to Israeli military occupation and opening up for free movement of people, would address both the issue of the right of return and of West Bank and Jerusalem settlements, the most intractable elements of the conflict. Both people's aspirations to have Jerusalem as their capital would also be addressed without infringing on the national or religious rights of either side, while the economic integration promised by Oslo could finally be achieved.

Also important, this scenario offers a way to bring an end to intercommunal conflict by meeting both communities' need for territory, sovereignty and security in the fullest, and fairest, way possible.

Incentives on both sides to resort to violence would thus be significantly reduced, while strong interstate institutions would ensure the protection of citizens regardless of whether they live in Jewish or Palestinian majority zones. And with the core issues resolved, a new and less confrontational regional geopolitical reality would finally be given room to emerge.

A Bold Vision

A parallel states scenario is certainly a radical departure from the territorially based, zero-sum notion of sovereignty that has grounded the nation-state for at least three centuries. But such a notion has not proved workable in Israel/Palestine, and its utility in the globalized era is even less apparent.

Of course, such an enterprise would pose unprecedented political challenges. But the difficulties entailed in establishing a parallel state structure would be far less than those posed by the two-state solution as presently conceived, or the alternative offered by its critics.

It's time to think outside the box and work toward a new, more holistic paradigm for resolving one of the world's longest ongoing ethno-national conflicts.

Indeed, parallel states offer benefits that other scenarios do not offer. It avoids the pitfalls of a single or binational state solution, in which Jews would lose political power as soon as Palestinians became the majority in the country, while eliminating the problem of creating a viable Palestinian state on the minimal territory currently left to them.

Is this a bold vision? Certainly. The question is whether it is less realistic than attempts at territorial division based on borders, whether those of 1967 or 1948, that have proved unable to bring real peace, security, or freedom for Israelis or Palestinians alike.

With other conceivable options fatally compromised, it's time to think outside the box and work toward a new, more holistic paradigm for resolving one of the world's longest ongoing ethno-national conflicts.

Hamas Must Be a Part of the Israeli-Palestinian Peace Process

Efraim Halevy

Efraim Halevy is a lawyer, former director of the Institute for Intelligence and Special Operations (Mossad), and former head of the Israeli National Security Council.

The current crisis in the [President Barack] Obama-[Israeli Prime Minister Benjamin] Netanyahu relationship should propel both leaders to reassess their basic policies toward Palestine. They must redefine their targets, to think realistically but also creatively.

Ending the conflict between Israel and Palestine is not an attainable goal. What is attainable is a clear and dramatic decrease in tension in the conflict—a goal that would, indeed, serve the necessities of American foreign policy on Iran, Afghanistan, and Yemen. Now is the moment to go back to the drawing board and to examine every option in search of a practical policy.

The Palestinian Authority and Hamas

For all their recent disagreements, Israel and the United States share a common view of the Palestinians. They have jointly affirmed their resolve to coax the Fatah-controlled Palestinian Authority (PA) to the negotiating table, while ignoring Hamas [Palestinian Islamic resistance movement]. This is a policy that has now lasted close to four years—with, by and large, the support of the international community. Hamas, it is commonly agreed, will only make an acceptable partner for negotiation if it undergoes an ideological transformation, a transformation that is very unlikely to ever occur.

But now might be the right time to reconsider this policy, especially in light of the recent behavior of the PA. To take one recent example: When the Israeli cabinet recently designated two sites in Hebron and Bethlehem to be preserved as national heritage landmarks, the PA joined Hamas in issuing inflammatory statements exhorting the populace to demonstrate against the Jewish appropriation of Muslim holy sites. Stone throwing and violence quickly ensued. Abu Mazen [also known as Mahmoud Abbas], the self-styled moderate president of the PA, provocatively warned of an impending religious war. Only a stern warning sent by Israeli security authorities brought the "moderate" Palestinian leadership to its senses. And even then, it was only the Israelis who were capable of becalming Jerusalem and the West Bank, with sustained and daily operations in Palestinian-controlled areas. In a time of crisis, the shortcomings of the ruling Palestinians were exposed.

The time has surely come to explore a new relationship with Hamas.

It can be difficult these days to distinguish the PA from its Hamas rivals in the West Bank. The festive inauguration of the Hurva Synagogue in the Jewish Quarter of Jerusalem's Old City brought nearly identical statements from the two groups. Just like the Hamas leader Khaled Meshaal, key members of the Palestinian Liberation Organization and aides to Abu Mazen argued that the reconstruction of this synagogue posed a serious threat to the Al-Aqsa mosque. It all raises the question: If the Palestinians in the West Bank won't make for good partners, then what?

The State of Affairs in Gaza

Gaza hardly seems a more promising place to answer this question, at least at first blush. Every time a rocket is launched from the strip, Israel holds Hamas responsible for the acts and justifiably retaliates. But Israel has also imposed an ironclad siege on Gaza—and, in so doing, it fails to acknowledge that Hamas also has a legal responsibility for the well-being of the ever-increasing population there.

What can change this state of affairs? The rump Palestinian Authority in Ramallah will never be able to restore its authority there. There's no sign that the population of Gaza intends to rebel against the Hamas regime. And nobody on the outside—not Israel, not the international community—has a coherent policy that will redress this situation. Thus, the people of Gaza are condemned to endure the present state of affairs indefinitely.

Under the current circumstances—with the destructive gamesmanship of the Palestinian Authority and the stagnation in Gaza—the time has surely come to explore a new relationship with Hamas. Attempts to penalize the group with exclusion have failed; perhaps, the time has come for a strategy that co-opts Hamas.

For starters, let's consider the prospect of a peace agreement between Israel and the Palestinian Authority that excludes Hamas. This would be a fool's errand. Hamas has a proven ability to play the role of spoiler, to exploit such a situation for its own political ends at the expense of peace. But we don't even need to progress that far in our thought experiment. Right now, the decaying Palestinian administration in Ramallah doesn't have the credibility to survive the rigors of negotiations, let alone the implementation of an agreement. Abu Mazen can only speak in the name of the West Bank, and recent events have shown that his mandate there is (at best) fragile.

Israel's current Palestinian strategy is not a winning one. That's because it has confined itself to playing a game with rules that place it at an inherent disadvantage. It must scramble these rules to have a chance. Bringing Hamas to the table would do just that.

The more that Hamas is permitted inside the tent, the better the prospects of a modest (yet historic) success.

The Benefits of Including Hamas

Hamas has demonstrated a will and a capacity to think and act pragmatically when it believes it useful or necessary. There's no better example of this than its governance of Gaza. Yes, it continues to play the role of peace-process spoiler when that role suits its interests. But Hamas has also demonstrated a serious capacity to exercise responsibility and restraint when that role suits its purposes. It has demonstrated its ability to control Gaza effectively, to both enforce a long-term cessation of hostilities and to withstand the combined efforts of the United States, Israel, and Egypt to bring it to its knees.

Before President Obama and [Prime Minister] Netanyahu proceed to negotiate with their dispirited Palestinian inter-locutors, why not reconsider the options? Bringing Hamas to the table could relieve pressure on the Palestinians—who would no longer need to worry about the Islamists attacking their credibility. It might create space for a less ideological approach to peacemaking, and it might allow for the negotiation of a more achievable agreement with Israel. Why not hammer out a temporary arrangement between the three sides that would, say, extend for 25 years with a clause for renewal? Such an agreement would make for a practical second-best outcome—a durable interim understanding.

Current policy, after all, sends Hamas the signal that it is doomed to exclusion come what may and forever. But the more that Hamas is permitted inside the tent, the better the prospects of a modest (yet historic) success. Of course, there will be those who say this is impossible. They will say Hamas is inhuman, and why would the Iranians ever allow this? The answer is that Fatah hardly behaves much better than Hamas. Besides, Fatah has limited ability to deliver any sort of peace without the consent of Hamas. As far as the Iranians go, once you start talking with Hamas, you soon discover how much they hate the guts of those renegade Shiites in Tehran. I could be wrong about all of this. But given the unworkable alternatives, surely this is worth putting to the test.

Hamas Has Proven Incapable of Joining the Israeli-Palestinian Peace Process

Michael Herzog

Michael Herzog, a retired brigadier general in the Israel Defense Forces (IDF), is the Israel-based Milton Fine International Fellow of the Washington Institute for Near East Policy.

In the four years since it swept Palestinian parliamentary elections, Hamas [a Palestinian Islamic resistance movement] has neither moderated its policies nor adopted democratic principles. Constantly torn between its ideology as an Islamist jihad movement and its responsibilities as a governing authority in the Gaza Strip, Hamas has proven unwilling to transform itself. The result has been an ongoing ideological and political crisis for Hamas and, more generally, the Palestinian Authority. Last October [2009] Hamas was faced with the challenge of new elections mandated by Palestinian law and set for January by the Palestinian Authority president, Mahmoud Abbas [also known as Abu Mazen], whose Fatah faction is Hamas' chief rival. Hamas' reaction was to ban any voting from taking place in Gaza. Consequently, Abbas postponed the elections indefinitely, sparking heated debate with Hamas over the legitimacy of his continued tenure as president.

The End of the Unity Government

Soon after Hamas' 2006 electoral victory, I identified some conditions necessary for co-opting ideologically extreme and violent political movements. I argued that Hamas was unlikely

Michael Herzog, "The Hamas Conundrum: The Untamed Shrew, Four Years On," *Foreign Affairs*, February 8, 2010. www.foreignaffairs.com. Copyright © 2010 by the Council on Foreign Affairs. All rights reserved. Reprinted by permission of FOREIGN AFFAIRS.

to become more moderate in the foreseeable future, primarily because there was neither a strong Palestinian government nor a viable political center capable of containing and co-opting the group. Unfortunately, this has proven to be true—and it remains so today.

After winning the 2006 election, Hamas immediately began grappling with various conflicting pressures. The Israeli government, which evacuated its citizens and military from Gaza in 2005, reacted strongly—militarily, economically, and diplomatically—to the continued firing of rockets from Gaza into southern Israel, first by factions other than Hamas and later by Hamas itself. Meanwhile, immediately after Hamas' electoral victory, the Quartet (the United States, the European Union, the United Nations, and Russia) demanded that Hamas, in order to gain international legitimacy, commit to non-violence, recognize Israel, and accept previous agreements signed between Israel and the Palestinian Authority. All the while, Hamas felt a domestic imperative to secure Palestinian national unity. In the face of these pressures, it consistently tried to govern without moderating its ideology. It remained dedicated to "resistance" and to Israel's destruction—and therefore opposed to any concept of a real peace process.

When forced to make hard choices, Hamas has been repeatedly pulled down by the weight of its dogma. In early 2007, in an attempt to halt escalating intra-Palestinian bloodshed and secure international aid, Hamas agreed to share power with Fatah in a national unity government. But Hamas adamantly refused to include in the government's platform any acceptance of the Quartet's conditions or of the 2002 Arab peace initiative, which proposed that Arab states normalize relations with Israel following a comprehensive settlement of Arab-Israeli issues. By June 2007, the national unity government had collapsed. Under the initiative of its more radical military wing, Hamas forcibly overran Gaza and brutally established its rule, in many cases throwing Fatah members from rooftops or shooting them in the knees. Thus, despite the expectations of some who encouraged Hamas' participation in politics, political inclusion did not contain or domesticate the group. Rather, Hamas resisted domestication until finally bursting out and forming an independent political entity.

The violent end of the unity government split the Palestinian territories into two entities—one in the West Bank, one in the Gaza Strip—with vastly different governments and political climates. In the West Bank, Abbas and Salam Fayyad, the Palestinian Authority prime minister, embarked on an overdue and unprecedented reform process, which included clamping down on Hamas grassroots groups through widespread arrests, the discharging of radical preachers from mosques, and the seizure of Hamas funds. The reform effort has brought improved security and impressive economic growth to the West Bank. In Gaza, by contrast, Hamas focused on being the flag-bearer for Islamists in the Middle East. This attitude led the group to cast aside practical realities in favor of pursuing ideological goals. In addition to forcing itself on local clans and usurping traditional power bases, Hamas initiated a gradual yet determined process of Islamization in all spheres of life. These included legislation and the courts; the education system; the media; and social life, as the group, in accordance with its Islamic code of conduct, demanded "modest" dress for women, banned mixed-gender social events, closed or monitored Internet cafés, and even condemned chewing gum because it "arouses the passion of the youth." Hamas' Islamization has also meant the systematic persecution of Gaza's Christians. As Abbas recently put it, Hamas' policies turned Gaza into "an emirate of darkness."

No Signs of Moderation

Despite this record, debate still persisted among Western commentators over whether Hamas was becoming moderate. This was because Hamas performed some window dressing to maintain its domestic legitimacy and garner international approval. Over the last two years, it has been conducting intermittent national unity talks with Fatah (to no avail). It also reached out to the West, suggesting a dialogue with Western governments. And some Hamas leaders occasionally expressed willingness to accept a long-term cease-fire with Israel if a Palestinian state were established along the 1967 borders. Hamas assumed these seemingly moderate postures as a way to address political pressures without reforming its ideology: There has been no evidence that Hamas leaders are reconsidering their core beliefs—only that they are, at most, debating which tactics best serve those beliefs.

Hamas cannot be part of an Israeli-Palestinian peace process based on recognizing Israel and making historic compromises, nor part of a Palestinian body politic based on democracy and free elections.

After Israel's pullout from Gaza, one of Hamas' main tactics was to allow, and later orchestrate, the regular firing of rockets from Gaza into nearby Israeli towns. Eventually, in December 2008, this rocket fire provoked Israel to launch Operation Cast Lead, a massive military operation in Gaza. It dealt a crippling blow to Hamas and deterred further rocket fire: Whereas 7,000 rockets and mortar shells were fired into Israel in the three years before the operation, only about 300 were fired in the 12 months following January 2009, as Hamas has enforced a near-total cease-fire since Operation Cast Lead ended that month.

At the same time, however, Hamas has been rearming, especially with long-range rockets, despite enhanced Egyptian efforts to curb the smuggling of weapons through tunnels under the Egypt-Gaza border. Hamas is helped in this smuggling effort by Iran. In October 2009, Hamas test-fired an Iranian-manufactured rocket capable of hitting Israel's largest city, Tel Aviv.

This history and the fact that the group seems to be ignoring strong pressures to reform—including rising domestic unpopularity and an unprecedented crisis in relations with Egypt—suggest that Hamas cannot be part of an Israeli-Palestinian peace process based on recognizing Israel and making historic compromises, nor part of a Palestinian body politic based on democracy and free elections.

Unless Hamas unexpectedly changes course, the group will exclude itself from the process.

Reaching a temporary cease-fire with Israel and claiming willingness to accept a Palestinian state within the 1967 borders is no true sign of moderation when Hamas is simultaneously building its arsenal and treating terrorism as a tactical tool. "Hamas will never give up the option of resistance," the Hamas political chief Khaled Mashaal stated at a rally last month [January 2010], "no matter how long it takes." Hamas' seemingly moderate political statements are always accompanied by forbidding conditions—for example, that in exchange for only a cease-fire on Hamas' part (not the recognition of Israel), Israel would have to withdraw to the 1967 lines and accept all Palestinian refugees.

Likewise, participating in the 2006 elections and flirting with national unity arrangements is not proof that Hamas has accepted the rules of democracy. The real test of a ruling party is if it agrees to a second round of elections, even if it might lose. Hamas failed that test recently when it undermined the scheduled Palestinian presidential and parliamentary elections.

Leaving Room for Peace

The sad conclusion is that Hamas presents one of those policy problems that are only manageable, not solvable. No force in Palestinian politics today has the power to break Hamas' ideological basis or grip on power in Gaza. For internal pressure to be effective—that is, for it to move Hamas to become more moderate, relinquish violence, endorse the peace process, and embrace democratic practices—it would have to be coupled with solid, sustained external pressure. If international powers, led by the United States and the other members of the Quartet, grant Hamas a free pass, the group will continue to play the spoiler, threaten Abbas and other moderates in the West Bank, and serve Iranian interests.

No matter what, changing Hamas will be a long-term journey, like any process of co-optation. The challenge is to manage it in a way that mitigates the impact on innocent Palestinians, minimizes the risk of all-out escalation, and leaves room for a viable peace process. These imperatives, in turn, underscore the urgency of relaunching the peace process under a supportive Arab umbrella that, based on shared concerns over Iran's bellicosity, would foster moderation and stability in the face of extremism. But the policy conundrum remains: Will the peace process progress with Hamas, or in spite of it? Unless Hamas unexpectedly changes course, the group will exclude itself from the process. That would be for the better. The challenge for policy makers in Washington, Europe, Jerusalem, and Ramallah then becomes how to deny Hamas the capacity to play the spoiler.

CHAPTER 3

Have US Military Actions in the Middle East Been Effective?

Overview: The Wars in Iraq and Afghanistan

Barack Obama

Barack Obama is the forty-fourth president of the United States, taking office in January 2009.

From this desk, seven and a half years ago [March 2003], President [George W.] Bush announced the beginning of military operations in Iraq. Much has changed since that night. A war to disarm a state became a fight against an insurgency. Terrorism and sectarian warfare threatened to tear Iraq apart. Thousands of Americans gave their lives; tens of thousands have been wounded. Our relations abroad were strained. Our unity at home was tested.

These are the rough waters encountered during the course of one of America's longest wars. Yet there has been one constant amidst these shifting tides. At every turn, America's men and women in uniform have served with courage and resolve. As commander in chief, I am incredibly proud of their service. And like all Americans, I'm awed by their sacrifice, and by the sacrifices of their families.

The Americans who have served in Iraq completed every mission they were given. They defeated a regime that had terrorized its people. Together with Iraqis and coalition partners who made huge sacrifices of their own, our troops fought block by block to help Iraq seize the chance for a better future. They shifted tactics to protect the Iraqi people, trained Iraqi security forces, and took out terrorist leaders. Because of our troops and civilians—and because of the resilience of the Iraqi people—Iraq has the opportunity to embrace a new destiny, even though many challenges remain.

Barack Obama, "Remarks by the President in Address to the Nation on the End of Combat Operations in Iraq," Whitehouse.gov, August 31, 2010.

The End of the Iraq War

So tonight [August 31, 2010], I am announcing that the American combat mission in Iraq has ended. Operation Iraqi Freedom is over, and the Iraqi people now have lead responsibility for the security of their country.

This was my pledge to the American people as a candidate for this office. Last February, I announced a plan that would bring our combat brigades out of Iraq, while redoubling our efforts to strengthen Iraq's security forces and support its government and people.

A transitional force of U.S. troops will remain in Iraq.

That's what we've done. We've removed nearly 100,000 U.S. troops from Iraq. We've closed or transferred to the Iraqis hundreds of bases. And we have moved millions of pieces of equipment out of Iraq.

This completes a transition to Iraqi responsibility for their own security. U.S. troops pulled out of Iraq's cities last summer, and Iraqi forces have moved into the lead with considerable skill and commitment to their fellow citizens. Even as Iraq continues to suffer terrorist attacks, security incidents have been near the lowest on record since the war began. And Iraqi forces have taken the fight to al Qaeda, removing much of its leadership in Iraqi-led operations.

This year also saw Iraq hold credible elections that drew a strong turnout. A caretaker administration is in place as Iraqis form a government based on the results of that election. Tonight, I encourage Iraq's leaders to move forward with a sense of urgency to form an inclusive government that is just, representative, and accountable to the Iraqi people. And when that government is in place, there should be no doubt: The Iraqi people will have a strong partner in the United States. Our combat mission is ending, but our commitment to Iraq's future is not.

103

The Transitional Mission

Going forward, a transitional force of U.S. troops will remain in Iraq with a different mission: advising and assisting Iraq's security forces, supporting Iraqi troops in targeted counterterrorism missions, and protecting our civilians. Consistent with our agreement with the Iraqi government, all U.S. troops will leave by the end of next year. As our military draws down, our dedicated civilians—diplomats, aid workers, and advisors—are moving into the lead to support Iraq as it strengthens its government, resolves political disputes, resettles those displaced by war, and builds ties with the region and the world. That's a message that Vice President [Joe] Biden is delivering to the Iraqi people through his visit there today.

This new approach reflects our long-term partnership with Iraq—one based upon mutual interest and mutual respect. Of course, violence will not end with our combat mission. Extremists will continue to set off bombs, attack Iraqi civilians and try to spark sectarian strife. But ultimately, these terrorists will fail to achieve their goals. Iraqis are a proud people. They have rejected sectarian war, and they have no interest in endless destruction. They understand that, in the end, only Iraqis can resolve their differences and police their streets. Only Iraqis can build a democracy within their borders. What America can do, and will do, is provide support for the Iraqi people as both a friend and a partner.

Ending this war is not only in Iraq's interest—it's in our own. The United States has paid a huge price to put the future of Iraq in the hands of its people. We have sent our young men and women to make enormous sacrifices in Iraq, and spent vast resources abroad at a time of tight budgets at home. We've persevered because of a belief we share with the Iraqi people—a belief that out of the ashes of war, a new beginning could be born in this cradle of civilization. Through this remarkable chapter in the history of the United States and Iraq, we have met our responsibility. Now, it's time to turn the page.

As we do, I'm mindful that the Iraq war has been a contentious issue at home. Here, too, it's time to turn the page. This afternoon, I spoke to former President George W. Bush. It's well known that he and I disagreed about the war from its outset. Yet no one can doubt President Bush's support for our troops, or his love of country and commitment to our security. As I've said, there were patriots who supported this war, and patriots who opposed it. And all of us are united in appreciation for our servicemen and women, and our hopes for Iraqis' future.

The greatness of our democracy is grounded in our ability to move beyond our differences, and to learn from our experience as we confront the many challenges ahead. And no challenge is more essential to our security than our fight against al Qaeda.

One of the lessons of our effort in Iraq is that American influence around the world is not a function of military force alone.

The War in Afghanistan

Americans across the political spectrum supported the use of force against those who attacked us on 9/11 [September 11, 2001]. Now, as we approach our 10th year of combat in Afghanistan, there are those who are understandably asking tough questions about our mission there. But we must never lose sight of what's at stake. As we speak, al Qaeda continues to plot against us, and its leadership remains anchored in the border regions of Afghanistan and Pakistan. We will disrupt, dismantle and defeat al Qaeda, while preventing Afghanistan from again serving as a base for terrorists. And because of our drawdown in Iraq, we are now able to apply the resources necessary to go on offense. In fact, over the last 19 months, nearly a dozen al Qaeda leaders—and hundreds of al Qaeda's extremist allies—have been killed or captured around the world.

Within Afghanistan, I've ordered the deployment of additional troops who—under the command of General David Petraeus—are fighting to break the Taliban's momentum. As with the surge in Iraq, these forces will be in place for a limited time to provide space for the Afghans to build their capacity and secure their own future. But, as was the case in Iraq, we can't do for Afghans what they must ultimately do for themselves. That's why we're training Afghan security forces and supporting a political resolution to Afghanistan's problems. And next August, we will begin a transition to Afghan responsibility. The pace of our troop reductions will be determined by conditions on the ground, and our support for Afghanistan will endure. But make no mistake: This transition will begin—because open-ended war serves neither our interests nor the Afghan people's.

Indeed, one of the lessons of our effort in Iraq is that American influence around the world is not a function of military force alone. We must use all elements of our power—including our diplomacy, our economic strength, and the power of America's example—to secure our interests and stand by our allies. And we must project a vision of the future that's based not just on our fears, but also on our hopes—a vision that recognizes the real dangers that exist around the world, but also the limitless possibilities of our time.

Post-War Priorities

Today, old adversaries are at peace, and emerging democracies are potential partners. New markets for our goods stretch from Asia to the Americas. A new push for peace in the Middle East will begin here tomorrow. Billions of young people want to move beyond the shackles of poverty and conflict. As the leader of the free world, America will do more than just defeat on the battlefield those who offer hatred and destruction—we will also lead among those who are willing to work together to expand freedom and opportunity for all people.

Now, that effort must begin within our own borders. Throughout our history, America has been willing to bear the burden of promoting liberty and human dignity overseas, understanding its links to our own liberty and security. But we have also understood that our nation's strength and influence abroad must be firmly anchored in our prosperity at home. And the bedrock of that prosperity must be a growing middle class.

Unfortunately, over the last decade, we've not done what's necessary to shore up the foundations of our own prosperity. We spent a trillion dollars at war, often financed by borrowing from overseas. This, in turn, has short-changed investments in our own people, and contributed to record deficits. For too long, we have put off tough decisions on everything from our manufacturing base to our energy policy to education reform. As a result, too many middle-class families find themselves working harder for less, while our nation's long-term competitiveness is put at risk.

And so at this moment, as we wind down the war in Iraq, we must tackle those challenges at home with as much energy, and grit, and sense of common purpose as our men and women in uniform who have served abroad. They have met every test that they faced. Now, it's our turn. Now, it's our responsibility to honor them by coming together, all of us, and working to secure the dream that so many generations have fought for—the dream that a better life awaits anyone who is willing to work for it and reach for it.

US Policy in the Middle East Has Yielded Good Results

George W. Bush

George W. Bush was the forty-third president of the United States, serving from 2001 to 2009.

From our earliest days as a nation, the Middle East has played a central role in American foreign policy. One of America's first military engagements as an independent nation was with the Barbary pirates. One of our first consulates was in Tangiers. Some of the most fateful choices made by American presidents have involved the Middle East—including President [Harry S.] Truman's decision to recognize Israel 60 years ago this past May [2008].

In the decades that followed that brave choice, American policy in the Middle East was shaped by the realities of the Cold War. Together with strong allies in the Middle East, we faced down and defeated the threat of communism to the region. With the collapse of the Soviet Union, the primary threat to America and the region became violent religious extremism. Through painful experience, it became clear that the old approach of promoting stability is unsuited to this new danger—and that the pursuit of security at the expense of liberty would leave us with neither one. Across the Middle East, many who sought a voice in the future of their countries found the only places open to dissent were radical mosques. Many turned to terror as a source of empowerment. And as a new century dawned, the violent currents swirling beneath the Middle East began to surface.

The Middle East at the Turn of the Twenty-First Century

In the Holy Land, the dashed expectations resulting from the collapse of the Camp David peace talks had given way to the second intifada. Palestinian suicide bombers struck with horrific frequency and lethality. They murdered innocent Israelis at a pizza parlor, or aboard buses, or in the middle of a Passover Seder. Israel Defense Forces responded with large-scale operations. And in 2001, more than 500 Israelis and Palestinians were killed.

Politically, the Palestinian Authority was led by a terrorist who stole from his people and walked away from peace. In Israel, Ariel Sharon was elected [prime minister] to fight terror and pursue a "Greater Israel" policy that allowed for no territorial concessions. Neither side could envision a return to negotiations or the realistic possibility of a two-state solution.

Elsewhere in the Middle East, Saddam Hussein had begun his third decade as the dictator of Iraq—a reign that included invading two neighbors, developing and using weapons of mass destruction, attempting to exterminate Marsh Arabs and many Kurds, paying the families of suicide bombers, systematically violating U.N. [United Nations] resolutions, and firing routinely at British and U.S. aircraft patrolling a no-fly zone.

Syria continued its occupation of Lebanon, with some 30,000 troops on Lebanese soil. Libya sponsored terror and pursued weapons of mass destruction. And in Iran, the prospect of reform was fading, the regime's sponsorship of terror continued, and its pursuit of nuclear weapons was largely unchecked.

Throughout the region, suffering and stagnation were rampant. The Arab Human Development Report revealed a bleak picture of high unemployment, poor education, high mortality rates for mothers, and almost no investment in technology. Above all, the Middle East suffered a deep deficit in freedom. Most people had no choice and no voice in choosing their leaders. Women enjoyed few rights. And there was little conversation about democratic change.

Against this backdrop, the terrorist movement was growing in strength and in ambition. [For] three decades, violent radicals had landed painful blows against America—the Iranian hostage crisis, the attacks on our embassy and Marine barracks in Beirut, the destruction of Pan Am Flight 103, the truck bombing of the World Trade Center, the attack on Khobar Towers, the bombing of our embassies in Kenya and Tanzania, and the strike on the USS *Cole*.

And then came September the 11th, 2001, when 19 men from the Middle East carried out the worst attack on the United States since the strike on Pearl Harbor 67 years ago this weekend [December 7, 1941]. In the space of a single morning, 9/11 etched a sharp dividing line in our history. We realized that we're in a struggle with fanatics pledged to our destruction. We saw that conditions of repression and despair on the other side of the world could bring suffering and death to our own streets.

An Offensive Stance on Terrorism

With these new realities in mind, America reshaped our approach to the Middle East. We made clear that we will defend our friends, our interests, and our people against any hostile attempt to dominate the Middle East—whether by terror, blackmail, or the pursuit of weapons of mass destruction. We have carried out this new strategy by following three overriding principles.

First, we took the offense against the terrorists overseas. We are waging a relentless campaign to break up extremist networks and deny them safe havens. As part of that offensive, we pledged to strengthen our partnership with every nation that joins in the fight against terror. We deepened our security cooperation with allies like Jordan and Egypt, and with our friends in the [Persian] Gulf. Saudi Arabia, long a breeding ground for radicalism, has become a determined partner in the fight against terror—killing or capturing hundreds of al Qaeda operatives in the Kingdom. We dramatically expanded counterterrorism ties with partners in North Africa. And we left no doubt that America would stand by our closest ally in the Middle East—the state of Israel.

Even though it required enormous sacrifice, we stood by the Iraqi people as they elected their own leaders and built a young democracy.

Second, we made clear that hostile regimes must end their support for terror and their pursuit of weapons of mass destruction, or face the concerted opposition of the world.

This was the approach we took in Iraq. It is true, as I've said many times, that Saddam Hussein was not connected to the 9/11 attacks. But the decision to remove Saddam from power cannot be viewed in isolation from 9/11. In a world where terrorists armed with box cutters had just killed nearly 3,000 of our people, America had to decide whether we could tolerate a sworn enemy that acted belligerently, that supported terror, and that intelligence agencies around the world believed had weapons of mass destruction.

It was clear to me, it was clear to members of both political parties, and to many leaders around the world that after 9/11, that was a risk we could not afford to take. So we went back to the United Nations Security Council, which unanimously passed Resolution 1441 calling on Saddam Hussein to disclose, disarm, or face serious consequences. With this resolution, we offered Saddam Hussein a final chance to comply with the demands of the world. And when he refused to resolve the issue peacefully, we acted with a coalition of nations to protect our people and liberated 25 million Iraqis.

When . . . Saddam's regime fell, we refused to take the easy option and install a friendly strongman in his place. Even though it required enormous sacrifice, we stood by the Iraqi people as they elected their own leaders and built a young democracy. When the violence reached its most dire point, pressure to withdraw reached its height. Yet failure in Iraq would have unleashed chaos, widened the violence, and allowed the terrorists to gain a new safe haven—a fundamental contradiction to our vision for the Middle East.

So we adopted a new strategy, and deployed more troops to secure the Iraqi people. When the surge met its objective, we began to bring our troops home under the policy of return on success. . . . Building on the gains made by the surge, the democratic government of Iraq approved two agreements with the United States that formalize our diplomatic, economic, and security ties and set a framework for the drawdown of American forces as the fight in Iraq nears its successful end.

After 9/11, we also confronted Libya over its weapons of mass destruction. The leader of Libya made a wise choice. In 2003, Colonel [Muammar al-]Gaddafi announced that he would abandon his weapons of mass destruction program. He concluded that the interests of his people would be best served by improving relations with America, and Libya turned over its nuclear centrifuges and other deadly equipment to the United States.

America is working to advance freedom and democracy as the great alternatives to repression and terror.

The defeat of Saddam also appears to have changed the calculation of Iran. According to our intelligence community, the regime in Tehran [the capital of Iran] had started a nuclear weapons program in the late-1980s, and they halted a key part of that program in 2003. America recognized that the most effective way to . . . persuade Iran to . . . renounce its nuclear weapons ambitions was to have partners at our side, so we supported an international effort led by our allies in Europe. This diplomacy yielded an encouraging result, when Iran agreed to suspend its uranium enrichment.

Sadly, after the election of President [Mahmoud] Ahmadinejad, Iran reversed course and announced it would begin enriching again. Since then, we've imposed tough sanctions through United Nations resolutions. We and our partners have offered Iran diplomatic and economic incentives to suspend enrichment. We have promised to support a peaceful civilian nuclear program. While Iran has not accepted these offers, we have made our bottom line clear: For the safety of our people and the peace of the world, America will not allow Iran to develop a nuclear weapon.

The Promotion of Freedom

Third, America identified the lack of freedom in the Middle East as a principal cause of the threats coming from the region. We concluded that if the region continued on the path it was headed—if another generation grew up with no hope for the future, and no outlet to express its views—the Middle East would continue to simmer in resentment and export violence.

To stop this from happening, we resolved to help the region steer itself toward a better course of freedom and dignity and hope. We're engaged in a battle with the extremists that is broader than a military conflict, and broader than a law enforcement operation. We are engaged in an ideological struggle. And to advance our security interests and moral interests, America is working to advance freedom and democracy as the great alternatives to repression and terror.

As part of this effort, we're pressing nations across the region—including our friends—to trust their people with greater freedom of speech, and worship, and assembly. We're giving strong support to young democracies. We're standing with reformers, and dissidents, and human rights activists across the region. Through new efforts like the Middle East Partnership

113

Initiative and the Broader Middle East and North Africa Initiative, we're supporting the rise of vibrant civil societies.

We're also advancing a broader vision that includes economic prosperity, quality health care and education, and women's rights. We've negotiated new free trade agreements in the region, supported Saudi Arabia's accession to the World Trade Organization, and proposed a new Middle East Free Trade Area. We have signed Millennium Challenge agreements with Jordan and Morocco to grant American assistance in return for anticorruption measures, free market policies, and investments in health and education. We're training Middle Eastern school teachers, translating children's school books into Arabic, and helping young people get visas to study here in the United States.

We're encouraging Middle Eastern women to get involved in politics, and to start their own businesses, and take charge of their health through wise practices like breast cancer screening. Efforts like these extend hope to the corners of despair, and in this work we have had a lot of help, but no finer ambassador of goodwill than my wife, Laura Bush.

The Israeli-Palestinian Conflict

Finally, to advance all the principles that I've outlined—supporting our friends, and pressuring our adversaries, and extending freedom—America has launched a sustained initiative to help bring peace to the Holy Land. At the heart of this effort is the vision of two democratic states, Israel and Palestine, living side by side in peace and security. I was the first American president to call for a Palestinian state, and . . . building support for the two-state solution has been a top priority of my administration.

To earn the trust of Israeli leaders, we made it clear that no Palestinian state would be born of terror, we backed Prime Minister Sharon's courageous withdrawal from Gaza, and we supported his decision to build a security fence, not as a political border but to protect the people from terror.

To help the Palestinian people achieve the state they deserve, we insisted on Palestinian leadership that rejects terror and recognizes Israel's right to exist. Now that this leadership has emerged, we're strongly supporting its efforts to build institutions of a vibrant democratic state.

While the Israelis and Palestinians have not yet produced an agreement, they have made important progress.

With good advice from leaders like former prime minister Tony Blair and Generals [James L.] Jones, [Keith] Dayton, [William] Fraser, and [Paul] Selva, the Palestinians are making progress toward capable security forces, a functioning legal system, government ministries that deliver services without corruption, and a market economy. In all our efforts to promote a two-state solution, we have included Arab leaders from across the region, because we fully understand that their support will be essential for the creation of a state and lasting peace.

Last fall at Annapolis, Israeli, Palestinian, and Arab leaders came together at an historic summit. [Palestinian Authority] President [Mahmoud] Abbas [also known as Abu Mazen] and [Israeli] Prime Minister [Ehud] Olmert agreed to launch direct negotiations on a peace agreement. Nations around the globe, including many in the Arab world, pledged to support them. The negotiations since Annapolis have been determined and substantial. Secretary [Condoleezza] Rice has encouraged both sides by hosting a series of trilateral meetings. And while the Israelis and Palestinians have not yet produced an agreement, they have made important progress. As they stated to the Quartet [United Nations, United States, European Union, and Russia], they have laid a new foundation of trust for the future.

On this issue—and on our overall approach to the Middle East these past eight years—America has been ambitious in vision, we have been bold in action, and we have been firm in purpose. Not every decision I've made has been popular, but popularity was never our aim. Our aim was to help a troubled region take the difficult first steps on the long journey to freedom and prosperity and hope. Some have called this idealistic, and no doubt it is. Yet it is the only practical way to help the people of the Middle East realize the dignity and justice they deserve. And it is the only practical way to protect the United States of America in the long term.

Signs of Progress in the Middle East

As with any large undertaking, these efforts have not always gone according to plan, and in some areas we've fallen short of our hopes. For example, the fight in Iraq has been longer and more costly than expected. The reluctance of entrenched regimes to open their political systems has been disappointing. There have been unfortunate setbacks at key points in the peace process—including the illness suffered by Prime Minister Sharon, the Hamas victory in the Palestinian elections, and the terrorist takeover of Gaza.

Despite these frustrations and disappointments, the Middle East in 2008 is a freer, more hopeful, and more promising place than it was in 2001.

For the first time in nearly three decades, the people of Lebanon are free from Syria's military occupation. Libya's nuclear weapons equipment is locked away in Oak Ridge, Tennessee. Places like the UAE [United Arab Emirates] and Bahrain are emerging as centers of commerce. The . . . regime in Iran is facing greater pressure from the international community than ever before. Terrorist organizations like al Qaeda have failed decisively in their attempts to take over nations. They're increasingly facing ideological rejection in the Arab world.

Iraq has gone from an enemy of America to a friend of America, from sponsoring terror to fighting terror, and from a brutal dictatorship to a multireligious, multiethnic constitutional democracy. Instead of the Iraq we would see if a Saddam Hussein were in power—an aggressive regime vastly enriched by oil, defying the United Nations, bullying its Arab neighbors, threatening Israel, and pursuing a nuclear arms race with Iran—we see an Iraq emerging peacefully with its neighbors, welcoming Arab ambassadors back to Baghdad, and showing the Middle East a powerful example of a moderate, prosperous, free nation.

At long last, the Middle East is closing a chapter of darkness and fear, and opening a new one written in the language of possibility and hope.

[On] the most vexing problem in the region—the Israeli-Palestinian conflict—there is now greater international consensus than at any point in modern memory. Israelis, Palestinians, and Arabs recognize the creation of a peaceful, democratic Palestinian state is in their interests. And through the Annapolis process, they started down a path that will end with two states living side by side in peace.

In fits and starts, political and economic reforms are advancing across the Middle East. Women have run for office in several nations and been named to important government positions in Bahrain and Oman and Qatar, the UAE and Yemen. Trade and foreign investment have expanded. Several nations have opened up private universities, and Internet use has risen sharply. Across the region, conversations about freedom and reform are growing louder. Expectations about government responsiveness are rising. And people are defying the condescending view that the culture of the Middle East is unfit for freedom.

There are still serious challenges facing the Middle East. Iran and Syria continue to sponsor terror. Iran's uranium enrichment remains a major threat to peace. Many in the region still live under oppression. Yet the changes of the past eight years herald the beginning of something historic and new. At long last, the Middle East is closing a chapter of darkness and fear, and opening a new one written in the language of possibility and hope. For the first time in generations, the region represents something more than a set of problems to be solved, or the site of energy resources to be developed. A free and peaceful Middle East will· represent a source of promise, and home of opportunity, and a vital contributor to the prosperity of the world.

US Military Presence in Iraq Has Been Effective and Is Still Needed

Kenneth M. Pollack

Kenneth M. Pollack is director of the Saban Center for Middle East Policy at the Brookings Institution. He is the author of A Path Out of the Desert: A Grand Strategy for America in the Middle East.

E*arly Thursday, less than two weeks before the president's Aug. 31 [2010] deadline for ending American combat operations in Iraq, the 4th Stryker Brigade, 2nd Infantry Division crossed the border from Iraq into Kuwait. With the departure of this last combat brigade, the U.S. military presence in Iraq is now down to 50,000 troops, fewer than at any time since the 2003 invasion. The shift offers a useful moment to take stock of both how much has been accomplished and how much is left to be done in what is fast becoming our forgotten war.*

The Myth of Troop Withdrawal

As of this month [August 2010], the United States no longer has combat troops in Iraq.

Not even close. Of the roughly 50,000 American military personnel who remain in Iraq, the majority are still combat troops—they're just named something else. The major units still in Iraq will no longer be called "brigade combat teams" and instead will be called "advisory and assistance brigades." But a rose by any other name is still a rose, and the differences in brigade structure and personnel are minimal.

American troops in Iraq will still go into harm's way. They will still accompany Iraqi units on combat missions—even if only as "advisers." American pilots will still fly combat missions in support of Iraqi ground forces. And American special forces will still face off against Iraqi terrorist groups in high-intensity operations. For that reason, when American troops leave their bases in Iraq, they will still, almost invariably, be in full "battle rattle" and ready for a fight.

What has changed over the past 12 to 18 months is the level of violence in Iraq. There is much less of it: The civil war and the insurgency have been suppressed and the terrorists have been marginalized, so American troops have been able to pass the majority of their remaining combat responsibilities to the Iraqi security forces. Most U.S. troops now have little expectation of seeing combat in Iraq. Instead, they are spending more time acting as peacekeepers, protecting personnel and facilities, and advising Iraqi formations. But that didn't start this month: It's more or less what they have been doing since the "clear and hold" operations to take back the country from militias and insurgents ended in 2008.

An ongoing American commitment to Iraq is so important.

The Risk of Civil War

Thanks to the troop "surge," Iraq is secure enough that it will not fall back into civil war as U.S. forces pull out.

Security in Iraq has improved enormously since the darkest days of 2005–2006, but the jury is still out on what will happen in the months and years ahead.

Extensive research on intercommunal civil wars—wars like Iraq's, in which a breakdown in governance prompts different communities to fight one another for power—finds a dangerous propensity toward recidivism. Moreover, the fear, anger, greed and desire for revenge that helped propel Iraq into civil war in the first place remain just beneath the surface.

Academic studies of scores of civil wars from the past century show that roughly 50 percent of the time, war will recur within five years of a cease-fire. If the country has major "lootable" resources such as gold, diamonds or oil, the odds climb higher still. The important bright spot, however, is that if a great power is willing to make a long-term commitment to serving as peacekeeper and mediator (the role the United States is playing in Iraq today), the recidivism rate drops to less than one in three. This is why an ongoing American commitment to Iraq is so important.

It's also worth pointing out that a civil war doesn't recur because the public desires one. Most people recognize that civil war is a disaster. Instead, such wars flare up again because leaders still believe they can achieve their objectives by force. Until they are convinced otherwise—ideally, by a great power's military forces—they will revert to fighting.

The Success of U.S. Strategy

The United States is leaving behind a broken political system.

If some on the right want to claim (incorrectly) that the surge stabilized Iraq to the point that civil war is impossible, their counterparts on the left try to insist (equally incorrectly) that the change in U.S. tactics and strategy in 2007–2008 had no impact on Iraq's politics whatsoever.

Partisans will debate the impact of the surge for years to come, and historians will take up the fight thereafter. However, Iraqi politics are fundamentally different today than they were in 2006. The nation's political leaders have been forced to embrace democracy—in many cases very grudgingly, but embrace it they have. Party leaders no longer scheme to kill their rivals, but to outvote them. They can no longer intimidate voters; they have to persuade them. And the smart ones have figured out that they must deliver what their constituents want, namely, effective governance, jobs, and services such as electricity and clean water.

Yes, Iraqi politics remain deadlocked and deeply dysfunctional, and yes, long-term stability and short-term economic needs depend on further political progress. But it is now possible to imagine Iraq muddling on toward real peace, pluralism and even prosperity—if it gets the right breaks and a fair amount of continuing help from the United States, the United Nations and its neighbors.

Iraqi Opinion on U.S. Troops

Iraqis want U.S. troops to stay. Or they want them to leave.

Be very, very careful with Iraqi public opinion. Polls are rarely subtle enough to capture the complexity of Iraqi views. Typically, they show a small number of Iraqis who want the Americans out immediately at any cost, a small number who want them to stay forever and a vast majority in the middle—determined that U.S. troops should leave, but only after a certain period of time. When Iraqis are asked how long they believe our troops are needed, their answers range from a few months to a few years, but are strongly linked to however long the respondent believes it will take Iraq's forces to be able to handle security on their own.

Going forward, America's involvement in Iraq can (and hopefully will) be much reduced, but the need for a U.S. presence will endure for many years.

One typically hears the same from people across Iraq and throughout its social and political strata. Iraqis are nationalistic, and they resent the American military presence. Many are also bitter over the mess that the United States made by invading and then failing to secure the country or to begin a comprehensive rebuilding process, failures that led to civil war in 2005–2006. Most Iraqis are relieved to have been rescued from that descent and are frightened that it will resume when the Americans leave. This is because their security forces are still untested and their political process has yet to show the kind of maturity that would provide Iraqis confidence that they are safe from the threat of more civil war. Consequently, a great many people are both determined to see all American troops leave—and terrified that they actually will.

The U.S. Time Line in Iraq

The war will end "on schedule."

Much as we should want the Obama administration to succeed in Iraq, this statement by the president in a speech to veterans this month should make us wary. If uttered in the first act of a Greek tragedy, it is exactly the kind of claim that would end in a Sophoclean fall.

As George W. Bush learned to his dismay, once you start a war, a lot of bad, unpredictable things can happen. No war has ever gone precisely according to schedule, not even those that have ended in the most dramatic victories, such as Israel's Six-Day War or the Persian Gulf War. What's more, war's aftereffects linger for many years.

Going forward, America's involvement in Iraq can (and hopefully will) be much reduced, but the need for a U.S. presence will endure for many years. Iraq has demonstrated great potential, but at this point it is only potential. The country still holds great peril as well—not just for Iraqis, but for our interests in one of the world's most strategically important regions.

For these reasons, Obama was right to also warn that the United States will need to remain deeply involved in Iraq and will probably face casualties there in the years to come, regardless of how we label our mission.

US Military Presence in the Middle East Is Unnecessary and Counterproductive

Bradley L. Bowman

Bradley L. Bowman is a major as well as a strategic plans and policy officer in the United States Army.

The U.S. military presence in the Middle East has represented one of the leading sources of radicalization and terrorism directed against the United States. Yet, protecting U.S. interests in the region does not require an obtrusive U.S. military footprint characterized by sprawling bases occupied by large numbers of permanently stationed ground troops. In fact, a large U.S. military presence in the region is unnecessary and often counterproductive. If policy makers ignore the role of the U.S. military presence in the radicalization process and fail to assess the actual necessity of a large U.S. military presence, the United States will find itself in a needless predicament not unlike the Herculean struggle against the mythological hydra. For every Abu Musab al-Zarqawi [an al Qaeda leader in Iraq] that the United States kills, the continuing sources of radicalization will generate a virtually limitless pool of replacements. . . .

U.S. Interest in Oil in the Middle East

A successful military posture in the Middle East must be based on and intricately linked with U.S. interests in the region and the preeminent threats to those interests. Although protecting Israel and fostering friendly relations with moderate Arab governments are certainly important, the United

Bradley L. Bowman, "After Iraq: Future U.S. Military Posture in the Middle East," *Washington Quarterly*, vol. 31, no. 2, Spring 2008, pp. 77–91. Copyright © 2008 by the Center for Strategic and International Studies (CSIS) and the Massachusetts Institute of Technology. All rights reserved. Reproduced by permission.

States' most vital interests in the Middle East are reliable access to Persian Gulf oil, counter-proliferation, and counterterrorism.

The need for a reliable and unimpeded flow of oil from the Persian Gulf region to the United States and other industrialized countries represents the first and longest-standing vital U.S. interest in the Middle East. Despite renewed conservation and alternative energy initiatives, the Energy Information Administration (EIA) forecasts a 71 percent increase in world energy consumption from 2003 to 2030, with petroleum continuing to satisfy most of this demand. Between 2005 and 2030, the EIA predicts that global and U.S. petroleum consumption will increase 39 percent and 23 percent, respectively. The United States currently imports roughly 60 percent of the oil that it consumes, and the EIA expects this U.S. dependence on foreign oil imports to increase to 62 percent of consumption by 2030. The energy suppliers of the Persian Gulf region will play a central role in satisfying this growing demand for the foreseeable future. In 2003, these countries accounted for 27 percent of the world's oil production and controlled 57 percent of the world's proven crude oil reserves and 41 percent of the world's natural gas reserves. By 2020, the Persian Gulf's contribution to global oil production is expected to rise to 33 percent. If the U.S. or the global economy were deprived of this oil or natural gas, the economic and political consequences would be devastating and far-reaching.

Terrorists or hostile states could threaten Persian Gulf oil flows in three ways: domestic stability, land-based infrastructure, and maritime assets. A successful revolution or widespread instability in a major oil producing country such as Saudi Arabia could endanger U.S. access to a large portion of its Middle Eastern oil imports. During the first five months of 2005, Saudi Arabia provided 14.9 percent of U.S. crude oil imports. Second, the region's land-based oil industry infrastructure, consisting of pipelines, oil refineries, and processing plants, presents another area of vulnerability. Egypt's Sumed pipeline and Saudi Arabia's Abqaiq processing facility present particularly attractive terrorist targets. In February 2006, al Qaeda claimed credit for an attempted suicide attack on the Abqaiq plant. Although the attack caused little damage to the facility, this incident demonstrates al Qaeda's intent to attack oil infrastructure. Finally, roughly 17 million barrels, or two-fifths of all globally traded oil, flows through the Strait of Hormuz every day. States such as Iran or terrorist groups such as al Qaeda could threaten the oil flow through the Strait of Hormuz or other key waterways such as Bab el-Mandeb, which connects the Red Sea with the Gulf of Aden and the Arabian Sea. Captured al Qaeda manuals reveal sophisticated instructions and advice for conducting maritime attacks on oil and natural gas tankers.

U.S. Interest in Reducing Weapons and Terrorism

The second highly important interest of the United States in the Middle East is to ensure that state and non-state actors in the region do not develop, obtain, or use weapons of mass destruction (WMD). Although the threats posed by biological and chemical weapons also warrant the attention of policy makers, nuclear weapons are unique in their ability to inflict casualties on a catastrophic scale. In the Middle East today, Iran presents the most serious threat to U.S. efforts to stop nuclear weapons proliferation. At worst, Tehran [the capital of Iran] could use its nuclear weapons to launch a first strike against Israel or could deliberately and covertly give nuclear weapons–related technology or materials to terrorist groups such as Hizballah to strike Israel and U.S. interests while minimizing the obvious fingerprints that would invite retaliation.

Although these concerns should not be prematurely discounted, little evidence exists to suggest that Iran would take such steps that would virtually guarantee Iran's destruction. Iranian development of nuclear weapons, however, would most likely lead to a more aggressive Iranian foreign policy, could potentially spark a regional nuclear arms race, and would increase the likelihood that nuclear technology or materials could inadvertently end up in the hands of terrorist groups such as Hizballah or al Qaeda. Given the nature of the Iranian political and military establishment, it is entirely plausible that a disenchanted, corrupt, or ideologically motivated group of actors could transfer key nuclear technology, materials, or weapons without the knowledge of the Iranian leaders, similar to [nuclear scientist] A. Q. [Adbul Qadeer] Khan's behavior in Pakistan. As more states obtain nuclear weapons and as nuclear technology and expertise become increasingly available, the chance that a nuclear transfer could lead to a successful attack against the United States and its friends increases.

The United States' third vital interest is fostering a region that does not spawn, suffer from, or export violent Islamist extremism. Al Qaeda and its associated terrorist movements represent the most serious threat facing the U.S. homeland and U.S. interests in the Middle East. The United States must therefore work with its regional partners to capture or kill violent Islamist extremists who threaten U.S. interests while addressing the causes of radicalization in the Middle East that are creating the next generation of Islamist terrorists.

U.S. Troops in the Middle East

During the Cold War [a period of mistrust between the United States and the Soviet Union, from 1947 to 1991], the presence of U.S. troops in the region was limited and infrequent. The United States deployed troops to Lebanon for a few months in 1958 and provided international peacekeeping forces in Lebanon (1982–1984) and the Sinai (1981–present). The U.S. Navy also patrolled the waters of the eastern Mediterranean, the

Persian Gulf, and the Red Sea throughout the Cold War, with the navy's most significant operation consisting of a 1987–1988 reflagging of 11 Kuwaiti oil tankers in order to protect them from Iranian attack. Other than these relatively minor deployments and operations, the U.S. military conducted no major interventions and maintained few permanent bases in the Middle East.

For nearly five decades prior to the Persian Gulf War, the United States worked through regional allies such as Saudi Arabia (1933–present) and Iran (1953–1979) to protect U.S. interests in lieu of maintaining a large, permanent military presence. During this period, the United States attempted to minimize Soviet influence in the region by supporting anti-Soviet governments with military and economic aid. By utilizing this strategy, the United States effectively protected its interests in the Middle East for nearly one-half of a century. As late as 1989, the United States had less than 700 military personnel in Bahrain, Kuwait, Oman, Saudi Arabia, and the United Arab Emirates (UAE) combined.

The United States needs only a minimal military footprint to counter threats to its three key interests.

Following Saddam Hussein's invasion of Kuwait in 1990, the United States deployed more than 500,000 military personnel to Saudi Arabia. This introduction of thousands of U.S. troops into Saudi Arabia represented a dramatic turning point in U.S. strategy and military posture in the region. In the wake of the Gulf War, the United States maintained a large military presence in Saudi Arabia and Kuwait, despite increasingly vitriolic calls for its departure. In an attempt to decrease the visibility of the U.S. footprint in the country, the military moved most of its forces to more remote locations in Saudi Arabia in 1996. Yet, this did not diminish widespread anger over the U.S. presence, as the Saudi regime saw it as an increasing liability.

Eventually, the September 11 [2001] attacks, the 2003 U.S.-led invasion of Iraq, and the subsequent overthrow of Saddam [Hussein] led to a significant reduction in U.S. military forces in Saudi Arabia. Currently, the United States maintains more than 220,000 soldiers, sailors, and marines in Iraq and the GCC [Gulf Cooperation Council] states: Bahrain, Kuwait, Oman, Qatar, Saudi Arabia, and the UAE. The bulk of these forces reside in Iraq and Kuwait as part of Operation Iraqi Freedom. As of September 2007, the United States maintained more than three times as many military personnel in Bahrain, Oman, Saudi Arabia, Qatar, and the UAE than it did in 1989.

Protecting U.S. Interests in the Middle East

Despite the U.S. military presence's dramatic growth in the Middle East since 1989, the United States needs only a minimal military footprint to counter threats to its three key interests. First, to guarantee a reliable flow of oil from the Persian Gulf region, the United States must promote domestic stability and protect land-based infrastructure as well as maritime assets. With respect to domestic instability or revolution, the U.S. military plays a limited role. If domestic instability or revolution threatens an oil-producing government, this is most effectively confronted by the respective government. Although U.S. special forces and intelligence services may assist covertly, in nearly every conceivable scenario, existing U.S. bases and conventional military forces offer little assistance and may actually exacerbate conditions by fomenting radicalism and popular unrest against the U.S. military presence and the host government that condones it. The United States should take nonmilitary steps in advance of such crises. By significantly reducing the U.S. military footprint that often fuels radicalization and by using U.S. political and economic power to encourage oil-producing governments to diversify their economies, invest in their people, and progress gradually toward constitutional liberalism, the United States can reduce the likelihood of domestic instability or revolution that would threaten an oil-producing ally. . . .

The second vital U.S. interest in the Middle East is to ensure that regional state and non-state actors do not develop, obtain, or utilize weapons of mass destruction. . . .

The U.S. military presence in Saudi Arabia certainly did not justify al Qaeda's tragic and immoral slaughter of nearly 3,000 innocent Americans, but it did largely explain it.

Some may attempt to justify an expansion of the U.S. military presence in the GCC states by arguing that a large network of U.S. bases manned by large quantities of U.S. troops would be necessary if the United States decided to attack Iran to prevent it from obtaining nuclear weapons. If Washington were to take this risky step, the most likely tactic would consist of precision strikes and limited incursions designed to eliminate Iranian nuclear facilities and retaliatory capabilities. The existing U.S. military infrastructure in the GCC is more than adequate to conduct and support such operations. Thus, even in the case of an ill-advised U.S. attack on Iran, an expansion of the U.S. military presence in the GCC states is not necessary. The U.S. military could launch these attacks from vessels in adjacent waters and from one or two air force bases on the periphery of the Middle East. If additional troops were required, the United States could quickly move them into the region from Europe or other locations, taking advantage of the increasing mobility and expeditionary nature of the U.S. military. These ground troops could arrive in a matter of hours or days and could quickly put into operation prepositioned equipment discretely stored throughout the region.

The third and final vital U.S. interest in the Middle East is the creation of a region that does not spawn, suffer from, or export violent Islamist extremism. Ironically, a robust U.S. ground troop presence in the region undercuts this interest, serving as a major impetus for radicalization. Yet, a large U.S. military presence is by no means the only source of radicalization and terrorism directed against the United States. Polling data and anecdotal evidence suggest that other factors, such as the Arab-Israeli crisis and the authoritarian nature of most Middle Eastern regimes, also play a role. Moreover, U.S. ground forces do have a constructive role to play in the region. The U.S. military can help train allied military forces to secure their borders, reduce "ungoverned areas," and confront insurgents or terrorist cells. The vast majority of this training, however, can occur out of the public eye using small, low-visibility U.S. military and CIA [Central Intelligence Agency] teams temporarily deployed to the region. Although a dramatic reduction in the number of permanently based U.S. troops in the Middle East would not immediately eliminate the threat from Islamist terrorist groups, it would significantly reduce the radicalization of future generations.

The Counterproductive U.S. Military Presence

Not only is a large U.S. military presence in the Middle East unnecessary, but it is also frequently counterproductive. A look at the rise of al Qaeda as a threat to the United States in the 1990s illustrates the radicalizing effect that often accompanies a U.S. military presence. The U.S. military presence in Saudi Arabia represents the primary reason Osama bin Laden and al Qaeda began to target the United States in the 1990s. As early as 1994, bin Laden publicly decried the U.S. military presence in Saudi Arabia. He followed these initial public condemnations with a message in 1996 entitled "Declaration of Jihad," stating that "the greatest disaster to befall the Muslims since the death of the Prophet Muhammad—is the occupation of Saudi Arabia, which is the cornerstone of the Islamic world, place of revelation, source of the Prophetic mission, and home of the Noble Ka'ba where Muslims direct their prayers. Despite this, it was occupied by the armies of the Christians, the Americans, and their allies."

Two years later, in February 1998, bin Laden joined Ayman al-Zawahiri and three other Islamist leaders from Bangladesh, Egypt, and Pakistan in issuing a formal declaration regarding the religious duty of Muslims to wage jihad against U.S. military personnel and civilians. After a paragraph of the requisite salutations and religious formalities, the authors immediately cite the preeminent reason for the jihad against the Americans: "Firstly, for over seven years America has occupied the holiest part of the Islamic lands, the Arabian peninsula, plundering its wealth, dictating to its leaders, humiliating its people, terrorizing its neighbors, and turning its bases there into a spearhead with which to fight the neighboring Muslim peoples."

A U.S. military presence is strongly correlated with the recruitment and motivation of al Qaeda's most radicalized members.

The U.S. military presence in Saudi Arabia certainly did not justify al Qaeda's tragic and immoral slaughter of nearly 3,000 innocent Americans, but it did largely explain it. From the perspective of bin Laden and a large segment of the Arab world, the United States was an occupying power in Saudi Arabia, and the only way to compel it to leave was for al Qaeda to use the only effective tool at its disposal: terrorism. Not only did bin Laden consistently cite the U.S. presence in Saudi Arabia as the paramount justification for jihad in the years leading up to the September 11 attacks, but 15 of 19 hijackers were from Saudi Arabia, two from the UAE, one from Egypt, and one from Lebanon. In a poll of Saudis taken after the September 11 attacks, 95 percent of Saudis agreed with bin Laden's objection to U.S. forces in the region. The centrality of the *Hejaz*, the area encompassing Mecca, Medina, and its surrounding areas, in the Muslim faith makes the presence of foreign troops in Saudi Arabia significantly more offensive compared to a troop presence in countries on Saudi Arabia's periphery. Consequently, the 2003 reduction of U.S. troops in Saudi Arabia represented a step in the right direction for the United States to address this source of radicalization.

The Increase in Radicalization

The 2006 U.S. "National Strategy for Combating Terrorism" largely neglects the role of the U.S. military presence in al Qaeda's emergence or in the continuing radicalization that fuels terrorism, pointing instead to social, political, and ideological maladies endemic to the Arab world, as well as past U.S. support for authoritarian regimes. Admittedly, there is rarely a single explanation for any phenomenon, and it would be extremely difficult to definitively and quantifiably rank the causes for al Qaeda's emergence and its attacks on the United States. Yet, for purposes of developing the future U.S. strategy and force posture in the region, one only needs to establish that the U.S. military presence was and continues to be one of a handful of major catalysts for anti-Americanism and radicalization.

Both the private words and the public actions of al Qaeda support this less sweeping yet equally important assertion. In July 2005, U.S. forces in Iraq intercepted a confidential letter from Zawahiri to Zarqawi, the leader of al Qaeda in Iraq. In this private letter presumably not intended for public dissemination, Zawahiri wrote, "The Muslim masses . . . do not rally except against an outside occupying enemy, especially if the enemy is firstly Jewish, and secondly American." Analysis of al Qaeda–connected terrorist attacks corroborates this revealing insight provided by al Qaeda's second-most senior leader. According to one study, the 71 al Qaeda operatives who committed suicide terrorism between 1995 and 2003 were 10 times more likely to come from Muslim countries where a U.S. military presence for combat operations existed than from other Muslim countries. Furthermore, when the U.S. military presence occupies a country with a larger proportion of Islamist radicals, al Qaeda suicide terrorists are 20 times more likely to come from that country. Although this evidence does not irrefutably demonstrate that the U.S. military presence in the Middle East is the leading source of radicalization, it suggests a U.S. military presence is strongly correlated with the recruitment and motivation of al Qaeda's most radicalized members.

The Iraq War Was
Unsuccessful and a Mistake

Malou Innocent

*Malou Innocent is a foreign policy analyst at the Cato Institute
and a member of the International Institute for Strategic Studies.*

There's a growing narrative that Iraq's solidifying democracy makes the seven years of US war and occupation a
worthy enterprise.

Some observers have even spun Iraq's March 7 [2010]
elections as proof that democracy promotion via military occupation can succeed. Don't believe the hype. The Iraq war remains a mistake of mammoth proportions. And Iraq's election
represents a pyrrhic victory, as the economic, political, and
moral costs of the occupation far outweigh any benefits.

The Costs of the Iraq War

First are the sacrifices in terms of blood and treasure. The
broad consensus is that the war has cost the US economy well
over $700 billion—with the meter still running. The Iraq war
has also left nearly 4,400 American troops dead, more than
31,000 physically disabled, and countless more psychologically
traumatized.

According to most estimates, more than 100,000 Iraqis
have been killed since the invasion. More than 2 million displaced Iraqi Sunnis, who fled into neighboring Jordan and
Syria, are adding instability to an already politically precarious
region of the world.

The war also upset the regional balance of power, as it
substantially strengthened Iran's influence in Iraq and severely

limited US policy options toward Tehran's clerical regime. No amount of prewar planning or "boots on the ground" could have prevented the Islamic Republic's political push into a neighboring country with a 60 percent Shiite majority. The removal of [Iraqi President] Saddam Hussein as the principal strategic counterweight to Iran paved the way for the expansion of Iranian influence in Iraq, and has enabled Tehran to back, with far greater impunity, its political allies in Baghdad.

Even before 9/11 [September 11, 2001, attacks on the United States], Iran possessed a budding nuclear program, the region's largest population, an expansive ballistic missile arsenal, and significant influence over the Lebanese Shiite group Hezbollah. By adding to that list enhanced political influence in Iraq, Iran can be somewhat more assertive geopolitically in the region, further limiting US policy options.

The Impact on America's Reputation

A third side effect of the war waged purportedly in democracy's name is that it came at the expense of America's already frayed reputation in the Muslim world. Far from being seen as a benevolent liberator, the United States was perceived as a blundering behemoth—and an abusive, hypocritical one to boot.

People of the region are well aware of Washington's policies toward Iraq in the decades preceding 9/11. Policy makers tacitly supported the Baath Party's suppression of the Iraqi Communist Party in 1963, and helped restore the Baathists to power after a takeover by pro-Nasser [referring to former president of Egypt Gamal Abdel Nasser] Arab nationalists in 1968. From 1980 to 1988, during the Iran-Iraq War, the Central Intelligence Agency and the Defense Intelligence Agency gave Hussein battle-planning assistance, satellite imagery, tactical planning for air strikes, and information on Iranian deployments.

As the *Economist* detailed last fall, torture became routine under the US-supported [Iraqi Prime Minister Nouri al] Maliki regime. Hussein-era tactics of censorship are also re-emerging. The government announced plans to censor imported books and the Internet, and rescind the protective anonymity of e-mailers and bloggers. These repressive policies are quite similar to those imposed by yet another US-supported dictator in the region: Egyptian President Hosni Mubarak. As modern-day Egypt and now Iraq demonstrate, countries with procedural elections yet devoid of liberal norms can merely be Potemkin villages masquerading as democracies.

A Mistake for Many Reasons

A fourth consequence of the war in Iraq—and one that should determine whether it is deemed a "success"—is that it did little to keep America safe from al Qaeda, the perpetrators of 9/11. In this respect, what makes "Bush's war" in Iraq arguably one of the biggest strategic blunders in US history is not just the litany of failures it caused but the opportunities America lost. The disaster in Iraq diverted badly needed intelligence assets, public attention, and congressional oversight from the forgotten war in Afghanistan.

Maybe that's why two GOP [Republican] members of Congress who recently visited the Cato Institute in Washington revealed that most Republicans on the Hill now believe the Iraq war was a mistake. They also said that "more than half the Republican caucus" believes the way the US began the Afghanistan war was a mistake. Today, polls show that most Americans say the invasion of Iraq was a "mistake" and "not worth it."

As defenders try to argue that the war was justified, the most important lesson we must take away is not that more troops, better tactics, and improved cooperation can produce success the next time around. Rather, it is that wars have the potential to expose the limits of military power and armed interventions should be undertaken only when absolutely critical to a nation's security.

Seven years later, let's hope Americans have learned the right lessons. Let's hope, too, that fortunes in the Middle East will turn for the better, not just for the US and its tarnished prestige, but for the millions of innocent civilians uprooted by conflict.

CHAPTER 4

Current
CONTROVERSIES

Should the United States Be Involved with Problems in the Middle East?

Overview: US Foreign Aid in the Middle East

Jeremy M. Sharp

Jeremy M. Sharp is a specialist in Middle Eastern Affairs for the Congressional Research Service, a legislative branch government agency that provides policy and legal analysis to committees and members of Congress regardless of party affiliation.

Congress both authorizes and appropriates foreign assistance and conducts oversight on executive agencies' management of aid programs. As the largest regional recipient of U.S. economic and military aid, the Middle East is perennially a major focus of interest as Congress exercises these responsibilities.

U.S. Foreign Aid in the Middle East

In the Middle East, the United States has a number of strategic interests, ranging from support for the state of Israel and Israel's peaceful relations with its Arab neighbors, to the protection of vital petroleum supplies and the fight against international terrorism. U.S. assistance continues to support the 1979 peace treaty between Israel and Egypt and the continued stability of the Kingdom of Jordan, which signed its own peace treaty with Israel in 1994. U.S. funding also has focused on strengthening Palestinian governance and civil society, and aid officials have worked to ensure that U.S. aid to the West Bank is not diverted to terrorist groups, such as Hamas, which controls the Gaza Strip. Since the attacks of September 11, 2001, the United States has established region-wide aid programs that increase the focus on democracy promotion and encourage socioeconomic reform in an attempt to undercut the forces of radicalism in some Arab countries.

Jeremy M. Sharp, "U.S. Foreign Assistance to the Middle East: Historical Background, Recent Trends, and the FY2011 Request," Congressional Research Service—CRS Report for Congress, no. RL32260, June 15, 2010, pp. 1–2, 15–16. Opencrs.com.

Despite changing geopolitical conditions, U.S. foreign aid to the Middle East has historically been a function of U.S. national security interests in the region. The United States has pursued a foreign policy that seeks stability in a region with abundant energy reserves but volatile interstate relationships. Policy makers have often employed foreign aid to achieve this objective. Foreign aid has been used as leverage to encourage peace between Israel and her Arab neighbors, while strengthening bilateral relationships between the United States and Israel and between the United States and moderate Arab governments. Foreign aid has worked to cement close military cooperation between the United States and governments in the region, discouraging local states from engaging in uncontrollable arms races. Economic aid also has had an underlying strategic rationale, as U.S. funds have been employed to promote development in an attempt to undercut radicalism in partner countries.

The degree to which foreign assistance has contributed to the achievement of U.S. objectives in the Middle East is difficult to measure, but the consensus among most analysts seems to be that U.S. economic and security aid has contributed significantly to Israel's security, Egypt's stability, and Jordan's friendship with the United States. The promise of U.S. assistance to Israel and Egypt during peace negotiations in the late 1970s helped to enable both countries to take the risks needed for peace, and may have helped convince both countries that the United States was committed to supporting their peace efforts. Excluding Iraq, Israel and Egypt are the largest two recipients of U.S. aid respectively.

Critics of U.S. Aid Policy

There is debate over using foreign aid more aggressively to pursue various objectives in the Middle East. Some critics of U.S. policy would like to see additional conditions placed on U.S. aid to Egypt, for example, to achieve greater respect for democracy and human rights in that country. Others favor using the aid program more assertively as leverage to restart the Middle East peace process. Some might urge that aid should be conditioned on demonstrable progress in extending full political and economic rights to women and religious minorities. Others, however, assert that the overt use of aid—or the threat of aid reductions—to promote democracy and reform in the Middle East region could lead to a backlash against the United States, as well as to democratic reformers in those countries.

The degree to which the United States promotes democracy, human rights, and reform across the Middle East has been the subject of vigorous debate.

Critics of U.S. aid policy, particularly some in the Middle East, have argued that U.S. foreign aid exacerbates tensions in the region. Many Arab commentators insist that U.S. assistance to Israel indirectly causes suffering to Palestinians by supporting Israeli arms purchases. Another common argument asserts that U.S. foreign aid bolsters autocratic regimes with similar strategic interests to the United States. Some observers have called U.S. aid policy "contradictory," accusing the United States of bolstering its ties with autocratic regimes through military assistance, while advocating liberalization in the region with less funds dedicated to reform and development aid. As noted above, however, other analysts believe aid has helped protect Israel's security and stabilize the region. . . .

U.S. Promotion of Democracy

Since the terrorist attacks of 9/11 and the U.S. invasion of Iraq in 2003, the degree to which the United States promotes democracy, human rights, and reform across the Middle East has been the subject of vigorous debate. Some experts argue that the United States should advocate strongly for democracy in the Arab world and beyond (such as in Iran) as a counterweight to anti-American extremism and acts of terrorism. Democracy advocates assert that the lack of good governance in the region is the reason why most Arab countries score low on various socioeconomic development indicators. They suggest that the key to the region's stability and prosperity, a key U.S. national security interest, is democratization, even if it entails the empowerment of certain Islamist movements that oppose peace with Israel and security cooperation with the United States.

On the other hand, foreign policy "realists" insist that the pursuit of U.S. strategic interests should be paramount in dealing with the region's authoritarian governments. Although most realists would likely encourage the United States to incorporate a reform strategy into its overall policy for the region, in their view, it should not supersede more vital U.S. goals, such as resolving the Arab-Israeli conflict. As the United States scales back its involvement in Iraq, some experts charge that, short of a policy or regime change, the U.S. government has limited ability to dramatically restructure a foreign nation's political system, particularly in the Middle East.

Overall, many experts have charged that the U.S. commitment to promoting democracy in the Arab world and in Muslim-majority countries has waned and realism has replaced idealism in U.S. foreign policy. Since the 2006 victory of Hamas in Palestinian Authority elections, the 2006 war in Lebanon, and public revelations of Iran's expanding nuclear program, the United States appears to have less aggressively pursued political reform as a counterweight to Islamist-inspired radicalism. Regional security issues are seen as having returned to the forefront of U.S. policy, as U.S. officials have concentrated more on revitalizing the peace process, stabilizing Iraq, winning the war in Afghanistan and Pakistan, and preventing Iran from developing nuclear weapons.

The Obama Administration Policy

Critics charge that the [Barack] Obama administration has downplayed the role of democracy promotion in U.S. foreign policy, while administration officials suggest that President Obama has attempted to strike a balance between the realist and idealist camps. Some observers believe that the administration has attempted to repair U.S.-Arab bilateral relations in the wake of the previous administration's "freedom agenda." In his June 2009 Cairo speech, President Obama remarked, "I know—I know there has been controversy about the promotion of democracy in recent years, and much of this controversy is connected to the war in Iraq. So let me be clear: No system of government can or should be imposed [upon] one nation by any other."

Events on the ground, particularly in Egypt where a possible succession to President [Hosni] Mubarak may occur in the near future, will continue to test the United States' commitment to promoting democracy in the region. Iran, where reformists continue to struggle against an alliance of clerical and military elites, is another country targeted for U.S. support.

The United States Should Promote Democracy in the Middle East

Shadi Hamid and Steven Brooke

Shadi Hamid is deputy director of the Brookings Doha Center and a fellow at the Saban Center for Middle East Policy at the Brookings Institution. Steven Brooke is a doctorate student in the Department of Government at the University of Texas.

U.S. democracy promotion in the Middle East has suffered a series of crippling defeats. Despite occasionally paying lip service to the idea, few politicians on either the left or right appear committed to supporting democratic reform as a central component of American policy in the region. Who can really blame them, given that democracy promotion has become toxic to a public with little patience left for various "missions" abroad? But as the [Barack] Obama administration struggles to renew ties with the Muslim world, particularly in light of the June 2009 Cairo speech, it should resist the urge to abandon its predecessor's focus on promoting democracy in what remains the most undemocratic region in the world.

Promoting democratic reform, this time not just with rhetoric but with action, should be given higher priority in the current administration, even though early indications suggest the opposite may be happening. Despite all its bad press, democracy promotion remains, in the long run, the most effective way to undermine terrorism and political violence in the Middle East. This is not a very popular argument. Indeed, a key feature of the post-Bush debate over democratization is an insistence on separating support for democracy from any

Shadi Hamid and Steven Brooke, "Promoting Democracy to Stop Terror, Revisited," *Policy Review*, no. 159, February 1, 2010. Copyright © 2010 by Policy Review/Hoover Institution Stanford University. All rights reserved. Reproduced by permission.

explicit national security rationale. This, however, would be a mistake with troubling consequences for American foreign policy.

Current U.S. Policy Priorities

The twilight of the [George W.] Bush presidency and the start of Obama's ushered in an expansive discussion over the place of human rights and democracy in American foreign policy. An emerging consensus suggests that the U.S. approach must be fundamentally reassessed and "repositioned." This means, in part, a scaling down of scope and ambition and of avoiding the sweeping Wilsonian tones of recent years. That certainly sounds good. Anything, after all, would be better than the Bush administration's disconcerting mix of revolutionary pro-democracy rhetoric with time-honored realist policies of privileging "stable" pro-American dictators. This only managed to wring the worst out of both approaches.

In an ideal world, there would not be a need to justify or rationalize supporting democracy abroad; the moral imperative would be enough.

For its part, the Obama administration has made a strategic decision to shift the focus to resolving the Israeli-Palestinian conflict, which it sees, correctly, as a major source of Arab grievance. This, in turn, has led the administration to strengthen ties with autocratic regimes, such as Egypt and Jordan, which it sees as critical to the peace process.

Some might see such developments as a welcome re-prioritization. However, by downgrading support of Middle East democracy to one among many policy priorities, we risk returning to a pre-9/11 [referring to the period before the September 11, 2001, attacks on the United States] status quo, where the promotion of democracy would neither be worn on our sleeve nor trump short-term hard interests. The "transformative" nature of any democracy promotion project would be replaced by a more sober, targeted focus on providing technical assistance to legislative and judicial branches and strengthening civil society organizations in the region. In many ways, this would be a welcome change from the ideological overload of the post-9/11 environment. But in other ways, it would not.

Those who wish to avoid a piecemeal approach to reform and revive U.S. efforts to support democracy often come back to invocations of American exceptionalism and the argument that the United States, as the world's most powerful nation, has a responsibility to advance the very ideals which animated its founding. These arguments are attractive and admirable, but how durable can they be when translated into concrete policy initiatives? In the wake of a war ostensibly waged in the name of democracy, can a strategy resting on gauzy moral imperatives garner bipartisan support and therefore long-term policy stability? In an ideal world, there would not be a need to justify or rationalize supporting democracy abroad; the moral imperative would be enough. But in the world of politics and decision making, it rarely is.

The Bush Administration's Project

After the attacks of September 11th, a basic, intuitive proposition surfaced—that without basic democratic freedoms, citizens lack peaceful, constructive means to express their grievances and are thus more likely to resort to violence. Accordingly, 9/11 did not happen because the terrorists hated our freedom, but, rather, because the Middle East's stifling political environment had bred frustration, anger, and, ultimately, violence. Many in the region saw us as complicit, in large part because we were actively supporting—to the tune of billions of dollars in economic and military aid—the region's most repressive regimes. The realization that our long-standing support of dictatorships had backfired, producing a Middle

East rife with instability and political violence, was a sobering one, and grounded the policy debate in a way that has since been lost. The unfolding debate was interesting to watch, if only because it contradicted the popular perception that Republicans were uninterested in the "root causes" of terrorism. In fact, they were. And their somewhat novel ideas on how to address them would begin to figure prominently in the rhetoric and policies of the Bush administration.

It is safe to say that the Bush administration's project to promote Middle East democracy failed.

In a landmark speech at the National Endowment for Democracy in November 2003, President Bush argued that "as long as the Middle East remains a place where freedom does not flourish, it will remain a place of stagnation, resentment, and violence ready for export." This theme would become the centerpiece of his inaugural and State of the Union addresses in early 2005. In the latter, the president declared that "the best antidote to radicalism and terror is the tolerance and hope kindled in free societies." In the summer of 2005, Secretary of State Condoleezza Rice told a Cairo audience that "things have changed. We had a very rude awakening on September 11th, when I think we realized that our policies to try and promote what we thought was stability in the Middle East had actually allowed, underneath, a very malignant, meaning cancerous, form of extremism to grow up underneath because people didn't have outlets for their political views." The aggressive rhetoric was initially supported by the creation of aid programs with strong democracy components such as the Middle East Partnership Initiative (MEPI).

But with a deteriorating Iraq, an expansionist Iran, and the electoral success of Islamist parties throughout the region, American enthusiasm for promoting democracy began to wane. One Egyptian human rights activist despondently told us in the summer of 2006 that Washington's rhetoric "convinced thousands that the U.S. was serious about democracy and reform. We also believed this, but we were being deceived." Perhaps the most disheartening sign of how far the democratic wave receded in the Middle East came during the 2007 State of the Union address. President Bush singled out "places like Cuba, Belarus, and Burma," for democracy promotion, all safely away from his chaotic, failing experiment in the Arab world.

It is safe to say that the Bush administration's project to promote Middle East democracy failed. It failed because it was never really tried. With the exception of a brief period in 2004 and 2005 when significant pressure was put on Arab regimes, democracy promotion was little more than a rhetorical device. But lost in the shuffle is the fact that one of the strongest rationales for the "freedom agenda"—that the way to defeat terrorism in the long run is by supporting the growth of democratic institutions—hasn't necessarily been proven wrong, nor should it be so readily discarded due to its unfortunate association with the wrong methods and messengers. But this is precisely what seems to have happened.

Critics of Democracy Promotion

In the Fall 2007 *Washington Quarterly*, Francis Fukuyama and Michael McFaul argued that "the loudly proclaimed instrumentalization of democracy promotion in pursuit of U.S. national interests, such as the war on terrorism, taints democracy promotion and makes the United States seem hypocritical when security, economic, or other concerns trump its interests in democracy, as they inevitably will." Around the same time, Thomas Carothers, writing in the *Washington Post*, was more explicit in wishing to disassociate supporting democracy from the fight against terror: "Democracy promotion will need to be repositioned in the war on terrorism, away from the role of rhetorical centerpiece. It's an appealing notion that democratization will undercut the roots of violent Islamic radicalism. Yet democracy is not an antiterrorist elixir. At times democratization empowers political moderates over radicals, but it can also have the opposite effect."

Carothers and others are correct that democracy is not, nor has it ever been, some kind of panacea. To embrace such lofty expectations will only hasten disappointment. Promoting democracy is a difficult business with risks and consequences, among them the chance that emerging or immature democracies might, in the short-term, experience increased political violence and instability. And lack of democracy cannot take the blame for those, like the July 7th [2005] London bomber Mohammad Sidique Khan, whose paths to terrorism began in the freest nations in the world. As the histories of some of these jihadists illustrate, powerful cultural and religious forces cannot be ignored.

Understanding the interplay between tyranny and terror can allow us to better judge . . . the place of democracy promotion in the hierarchy of national priorities.

That said, decoupling support for democracy from the broader effort to combat terrorism and religious extremism in the Middle East would be a costly strategic misstep. If there is indeed a link between lack of democracy and terrorism—and we will argue that there is—then the matter of Middle East democracy is more urgent than it would otherwise be. The question of urgency is not an inconsequential one. Most policy makers and analysts would agree that the region's democratization should, in theory at least, be a long-term goal. But, if it is only considered as such, then it will not figure high on the agenda of an administration with a whole host of other problems, both foreign and domestic, to worry about. However, if the continued dominance of autocratic regimes in the region translates into a greater likelihood of political violence and terrorism, then it becomes an immediate threat to regional stability that the U.S. will need to address sooner rather than later.

The Link Between Tyranny and Terror

It is worth emphasizing that democracy promotion does not involve only our relationships with authoritarian allies like Egypt, Jordan, or Saudi Arabia. Our ability and willingness to understand the relationship between autocracy and terror is also intimately tied to future success in Iraq. Drawing on captured documents previously unavailable to the public, a 2008 study by West Point's Combating Terrorism Center found that "low levels of civil liberties are a powerful predictor of the national origin of foreign fighters in Iraq." Of nearly 600 al Qaeda in Iraq fighters listed in the declassified documents, 41 percent were from Saudi Arabia while 19 percent were of Libyan origin. The study also notes that "Saudi Arabian jihadis contribute far more money to [al Qaeda in Iraq] than fighters from other countries." According to the Freedom House index, the Saudi regime is one of the 17 most repressive governments in the world. Because the kingdom brooks no dissent at home, it has, since the early 1980s, sought to bolster its legitimacy by encouraging militants to fight abroad in support of various pan-Islamist causes. Since the late 1990s, those militants have tended to target the United States. In other words, Saudi Arabia's internal politics can have devastating external consequences.

Democratic reform also holds out hope for confronting other Middle Eastern flash points. In recent years, the notion of incorporating violent political actors in nonviolent, democratic processes has gained some currency, particularly in light of the successful integration of insurgents in Iraq. Meanwhile, in the Palestinian territories, whatever else one wishes to say about Hamas, the group's electoral participation since 2006 has coincided with a precipitous drop in the suicide bombings that had long been their hallmark.

Recognizing the relevance of democracy to some of the thorniest Middle Eastern conflicts—whose effects reverberate to our shores—makes democracy promotion much harder to dismiss as a luxury of idealism and a purely moral, long-term concern. In short, understanding the interplay between tyranny and terror can allow us to better judge—and, if necessary, elevate—the place of democracy promotion in the hierarchy of national priorities.

A Key Component of Counterterrorism

De-emphasizing support for democracy, on the other hand, will have significant consequences at a time when Arabs and Muslims are looking to us for moral leadership and holding out great expectations for an American president who many continue to see as sympathetic to their concerns. Obama's Cairo speech, hailed throughout the Middle East, was a step in the right direction, but disappointment has since grown as the administration has failed to follow up with tangible policy changes on the ground.

Dropping democracy down on the agenda would ignore the fact that our ideals coincide with those of the majority of Middle Easterners who are angry at us not for promoting democracy, but because we do not. When we say we want democracy but do very little about it, our credibility suffers and we are left open to charges of hypocrisy. This credibility gap should not be dismissed. Ultimately, the fight against terror is not simply about "connecting the dots," improving interagency coordination, and killing terrorists; it is just as important to have a broader vision that addresses the sources of political violence.

Any long-term strategy must take into account an emerging body of evidence which shows that lack of democracy can be a key predictor of terrorism, and correlates with it more strongly than other commonly cited factors like poverty and unemployment. If understood and utilized correctly, democracy promotion can become a key component of a revitalized counterterrorism strategy that tackles the core problem of reducing the appeal of violent extremism in Muslim societies. It has the potential to succeed where the more traditional, hard power components of counterterrorism strategy have failed.

A new democracy promotion strategy in the Middle East should include a variety of measures.

The link between lack of democracy and terrorism also has consequences for American domestic politics. It provides a unifying theme for Democrats and Republicans alike, one that honors our ideals while helping keep us safe and secure. To the extent that politicians have had difficulty selling democracy promotion to the American people, the "tyranny-terror link" provides a promising narrative for U.S. policy in managing the immense challenges of today's Middle East. . . .

A New Democracy Promotion Strategy

A multitude of factors—economic, political, cultural, and religious—contribute to Islamic radicalism and terror. However, one important factor, and one that appears to have a strong empirical basis, is the Middle East's democracy deficit. Any long-term strategy to combat terrorism should therefore include a vigorous, sustained effort to support democracy and democrats in a region long debilitated by autocracy. Obviously, this is an enormous challenge and should not be taken lightly. However, abandoning such a critical task would mean more of the same—a Middle East that continues to fester as a source of political instability and religious extremism. And, in today's world, such instability, and the violence that so often results, cannot be contained; it will spill over and harm America and its allies.

A new democracy promotion strategy in the Middle East should include a variety of measures, including making aid to autocratic regimes conditional on political and human rights reforms; elevating democracy as a crucial part of all high-level bilateral discussions with Arab leaders; coming to terms with the inclusion of nonviolent Islamist parties in the political process; using membership in international organizations as leverage; increasing the budget for programs like the Middle East Partnership Initiative and the Millennium Challenge Account; deepening cooperation with the European Union to spread responsibility; and sponsoring initiatives that bring together Islamist and secular groups to forge inclusive pro-democracy platforms. The pace of democratization should take into account local contexts yet must maintain a consistent focus on expanding the rights of citizens, supporting the development of viable opposition parties, and moving toward free and fair elections.

But before moving in such a direction, the idea of Middle East democracy must be rehabilitated in the eyes of policy makers and the public alike. Absent a bipartisan political commitment, any new effort will falter. We realize that elevating democracy promotion will mean breaking with the last several decades of U.S. policy, which has relied upon close relationships with Arab regimes at the expense of Arab publics. But our long-term national security, as well as our broader interests in the region, demands such a reorientation. The first step, however, is to reestablish a consensus here at home on both the utility and value of democracy promotion. Once that happens, the discussion of how to actually do it can be conducted with greater clarity. If, on the other hand, we choose to continue along the current path—paying lip service to the importance of democracy abroad but doing increasingly less to actually support it—a great opportunity will be lost.

Turning away from the Arabs and Muslims who overwhelmingly support greater freedom and democracy will rob us of perhaps our strongest weapon in the broader struggle of ideas. For decades, the people of the region have been denied the ability to chart their own course, ask their own questions, and form their own governments. Lack of democratic outlets has pushed people towards extreme methods of opposition and made the resort to terrorist acts more likely. Recognizing this is a crucial step toward a sustained effort to promote Middle East democracy and represents our best chance at a durable and effective counterterrorism policy that protects our vital interests while remaining true to our ideals.

The United States Should Take Military Action in Iran

Daniel Pipes

Daniel Pipes is director of the Middle East Forum and Taube Distinguished Visiting Fellow at the Hoover Institution of Stanford University.

I do not customarily offer advice to a president whose election I opposed, whose goals I fear, and whose policies I work against. But here is an idea for Barack Obama to salvage his tottering administration by taking a step that protects the United States and its allies.

The Obama Presidency

If Obama's personality, identity, and celebrity captivated a majority of the American electorate in 2008, those qualities proved ruefully deficient for governing in 2009. He failed to deliver on employment and health care, he failed in foreign-policy forays small (e.g., landing the 2016 Olympics) and large (relations with China and Japan). His counterterrorism record barely passes the laugh test.

This poor performance has caused an unprecedented collapse in the polls and the loss of three major by-elections, culminating two weeks ago [January 19, 2010] in an astonishing senatorial defeat in Massachusetts. Obama's attempts to "reset" his presidency will likely fail if he focuses on economics, where he is just one of many players.

He needs a dramatic gesture to change the public perception of him as a light-weight, bumbling ideologue, preferably in an arena where the stakes are high, where he can take charge, and where he can trump expectations.

The Iranian Nuclear Threat

Such an opportunity does exist: Obama can give orders for the U.S. military to destroy Iran's nuclear-weapon capacity.

Circumstances are propitious. First, U.S. intelligence agencies have reversed their preposterous 2007 National Intelligence Estimate, the one that claimed with "high confidence" that Tehran [the capital of Iran] had "halted its nuclear weapons program." No one other than the Iranian rulers and their agents denies that the regime is rushing headlong to build a large nuclear arsenal.

Second, if the apocalyptic-minded leaders in Tehran get the Bomb, they render the Middle East yet more volatile and dangerous. They might deploy these weapons in the region, leading to massive death and destruction. Eventually, they could launch an electromagnetic pulse attack on the United States, utterly devastating the country. By eliminating the Iranian nuclear threat, Obama protects the homeland and sends a message to America's friends and enemies.

Public Opinion on Bombing Iran

Third, polling shows long-standing American support for an attack on the Iranian nuclear infrastructure:

- *Los Angeles Times*/Bloomberg, January 2006: 57 percent of Americans favor military intervention if Tehran pursues a program that could enable it to build nuclear arms.

- Zogby International, October 2007: 52 percent of likely voters support a U.S. military strike to prevent Iran from building a nuclear weapon; 29 percent oppose such a step.

- McLaughlin & Associates, May 2009: When asked whether they would support "using the [U.S.] military to attack and destroy the facilities in Iran which are necessary to produce a nuclear weapon," 58 percent of 600 likely voters supported the use of force and 30 percent opposed it.

- Fox News, September 2009: When asked, "Do you support or oppose the United States taking military action to keep Iran from getting nuclear weapons?" 61 percent of 900 registered voters supported military action and 28 opposed it.

- Pew Research Center, October 2009: When asked which is more important, "to prevent Iran from developing nuclear weapons, even if it means taking military action," or "to avoid a military conflict with Iran, even if it means they may develop nuclear weapons," 61 percent of 1,500 respondents favored the first reply and 24 percent the second.

Not only does a strong majority—57, 52, 58, 61, and 61 percent in these five polls—already favor using force, but after a strike Americans will presumably rally around the flag, sending that number much higher.

The time to act is now, or, on Obama's watch, the world will soon become a much more dangerous place.

The Time to Act

Fourth, if the U.S. limited its strike to taking out Iran's nuclear facilities and did not attempt any regime change, it would require few "boots on the ground" and entail relatively few casualties, making an attack more politically palatable.

Just as 9/11 [September 11, 2001, terrorist attacks on the United States] caused voters to forget George W. Bush's meandering early months, a strike on Iranian facilities would dispatch Obama's reckless first year down the memory hole and transform the domestic political scene. It would sideline health care, prompt Republicans to work with Democrats, and make the netroots squeal, independents reconsider, and conservatives swoon.

But the chance to do good and do well is fleeting. As the Iranians improve their defenses and approach weaponization, the window of opportunity is closing. The time to act is now, or, on Obama's watch, the world will soon become a much more dangerous place.

The United States Should Disengage from the Middle East

Leon Hadar and Christopher Preble

Leon Hadar is a research fellow. Christopher Preble is director of foreign policy studies at the Cato Institute as well as the author of The Power Problem: How American Military Dominance Makes Us Less Safe, Less Prosperous, and Less Free.

For many decades, successive U.S. administrations have defined U.S. national security interests in the Middle East as ensuring access to Middle East oil, containing any aspiring regional hegemonic powers, and limiting the proliferation of weapons of mass destruction. Washington has tried to achieve this complex set of goals primarily through a network of informal security alliances—especially with Israel, Saudi Arabia, and Egypt. Americans have also attempted to broker peace between the Israelis and the Palestinians; Presidents George H. W. Bush and Bill Clinton both viewed resolution of the conflict as a central component of U.S. policy in the Middle East and attempted to expand the American role in the peace process on the assumption that a resolution of the conflict would reduce the appeal of anti-Americanism and contain the radical forces in the region.

After 9/11 [September 11, 2001, terrorist attacks on the United States], U.S. strategy in the Middle East changed dramatically. George W. Bush came into office intending to make a sharp break from his predecessors, and 9/11 facilitated a shift toward using military might to transform the balance of power in the region. The new administration will likely choose between Bush's example, employing or threatening the use of force to topple obstreperous regimes, or else revert to the policies of his predecessors, cajoling and pleading with the region's leaders to make peace. Given that neither approach has advanced U.S. security and yet has been very costly, the better option would be to chart an entirely new course.

U.S. Policy in the Middle East

Countries in the Middle East receive a disproportionate share of U.S. aid. The leading recipient of aid is Israel, but several other countries in the region, including Egypt and Jordan, are awarded hundreds of millions of dollars annually from U.S. taxpayers. The Near East region as a whole, which includes North Africa and the Persian Gulf States, received $5.26 billion in 2008, more than all of Africa, and nearly eight times the amount of aid delivered to East Asia.

The costs of U.S. policy in the Middle East are not confined to foreign aid, however. Economists have calculated that the deployment of the U.S. military to safeguard oil supplies from Saudi Arabia and the rest of the Persian Gulf—particularly since the first Gulf War—costs the United States between $30 billion and $60 billion a year. That calculation does not reflect the costs of the war against Iraq and the continuing occupation of that country. And no statistic can capture the high costs America is paying in the form of extreme anti-Americanism among Arabs and Muslims because of Washington's support for Israel and Saudi Arabia. The stationing of U.S. forces in Saudi Arabia after the first Gulf War is known to have stirred such deep hostility that Osama bin Laden made it the initial focus in his campaign to recruit Muslims from around the globe to attack Americans.

Unfortunately, the Bush administration's move to end the deployment of U.S. troops in Saudi Arabia in August 2003 was not part of an American strategy to disengage from the region, but rather was intended to relieve some of the political pressure on the Saudi royal family. As long as Washington continues to cling to the assumption that it must maintain a dominant military posture in the Persian Gulf, it will be unable to resolve the dilemmas it is currently facing. The alliance with the ruling Arab regimes and the U.S. military presence in the region will continue to foster anti-Americanism and may force the United States into more costly military engagements. Meanwhile, an effort to accelerate "democratization" would likely fail in the near term and could pose a very serious threat to U.S. security in the medium to long term. Given the virulent anti-American sentiments in Saudi Arabia and throughout the Middle East, a government that represented the wishes of the Saudi people could well choose to support al Qaeda or other anti-American terrorist groups.

U.S. Involvement in the Israeli-Palestinian Peace Process

The first President Bush convened the Madrid Peace Conference in October 1991, while the Clinton administration backed direct negotiations between Israel and Palestine. These negotiations led to the 1993 Oslo Accord between Israel and the Palestinian Liberation Organization and to a peace accord between Israel and Jordan. However, President Clinton's attempts at mediating a comprehensive peace accord between Israel and the Palestinians during the 2000 Camp David peace summit failed. The core issues—the future of the Jewish settlements in occupied Arab territories, the fate of Jerusalem and its holy sites, and the "right of return" demanded by Palestinian refugees that had left Israel in 1948—remained unresolved. Furthermore, the breakdown of U.S.-led negotiations produced a backlash in Israel where Ariel Sharon was elected prime minister in 2001, and in the Palestinian territories where Hamas gained ground against the more moderate Fatah. This set the stage for a new Palestinian uprising and the continuance of the vicious circle of anti-Israeli terrorism, accompanied by Israeli military retaliation.

The collapse of the Camp David talks and the start of the second intifada, followed by 9/11, demonstrated the high costs Americans would have to pay to maintain a dominant position in the Middle East, both as a military power and as a promoter of the peace process. Thus, in the aftermath of 9/11, policy makers advanced two alternative approaches.

The Bush administration's approach combined accelerated democratization and peacemaking, but these goals proved incompatible.

On the one hand, then secretary of state Colin Powell argued that by re-embracing the activist pro-Mideast peace process diplomacy of his predecessors, and by asserting U.S. leadership in a new international effort to revive Israeli-Palestinian negotiations, Washington could counter anti-Americanism and stabilize its position in the region. In particular, Powell promoted the Roadmap for Peace, presented by the "Quartet" of the United States, the European Union [EU], Russia, and the United Nations [UN] on September 17, 2002. Powell also wanted to provide support for the Arab peace initiative proposed by then crown prince Abdullah of Saudi Arabia in the Beirut summit on March 28, 2002. The initiative spelled out a "final-status agreement" whereby the members of the Arab League would offer full normalization of relations with Israel in exchange for the withdrawal of its forces from all occupied territories to UN borders established before the 1967 war, and a recognition of an independent Palestinian state with East Jerusalem as its capital.

A competing point of view held that the promotion of Israeli-Palestinian peace should be placed on the policy back burner while American military power would be applied against radical players in the region, including Iraq and Iran. Officials in Washington assumed that the establishment of pro-American democratic governments in Baghdad and other

Middle Eastern capitals would create conditions conducive to achieving Israeli-Palestinian peace. This alternative approach gained steam after 9/11. Israel was subjected to Palestinian terrorist attacks during the second intifada, and was considered a strategic ally of the United States in the war on terrorism and against rogue Middle Eastern regimes. Meanwhile, the Palestinian leadership, especially Palestinian Liberation Organization leader Yasser Arafat, was tainted with a stigma of terrorism.

Democratization and Peacemaking

The tilt toward Israel was revealed in 2002 when George W. Bush met several times with Israeli Prime Minister Ariel Sharon, whom he called "a man of peace," and repeatedly refused to meet with Arafat. Bush gave Sharon a green light to launch a large-scale Israeli military operation in the West Bank in March 2002, in response to a terrorist attack in the Israeli coastal city of Netanya. He also backed Tel Aviv's decision to construct a security fence in the West Bank and to withdraw its troops from the Gaza Strip.

Bush's policies eroded U.S. power and influence.

The Bush administration's approach combined accelerated democratization and peacemaking, but these goals proved incompatible. While Washington wanted new Palestinian leaders who would make peace with Israel under American supervision, several knowledgeable observers predicted that free elections in the Palestinian territories were likely to elevate anti-Israel forces to power.

And indeed that is exactly what happened with the Palestinian parliamentary elections in January 2006. The radical Islamist Hamas movement, bitterly anti-American and unremittingly hostile toward the peace process, defeated the more moderate but corrupt Fatah movement, winning a majority in the Palestinian Legislative Council. Despite the fact that Washington had pushed Palestinian President Mahmoud Abbas [also known as Abu Mazen] to hold the elections, U.S. policy makers belatedly reversed course. Washington refused to recognize the newly elected government and, together with Israel and the European Union, cut off all funds to the Palestinian Authority, insisting that economic aid to the Palestinians would be resumed only after Hamas ended violence and recognized Israel. The American and Israeli governments also encouraged the Fatah leadership to form a separate Palestinian government in the West Bank in June 2007 while Hamas remained in control of the Gaza Strip, a messy divorce that precipitated frequent violent clashes between Hamas and Fatah forces. Israeli forces and Hamas guerrillas, meanwhile, continued to exchange fire through 2008, although Egyptian mediation helped broker a cease-fire between the two sides in June 2008.

Washington's abortive attempt to implant democracy in Palestine as a means of creating conditions for peace in the Middle East reveals how U.S. policies have often worked at cross-purposes. The ousting of Saddam Hussein and the coming to power of a Shiite-controlled government in Baghdad helped tilt the balance of power in the Persian Gulf to Iran, a country that does not recognize Israel and opposes the peace process. In the Levant, in addition to the Hamas victory in the Palestinian elections in early 2006, a series of other developments that were initially welcomed by the Bush administration (for example, the parliamentary elections in Lebanon and the 2006 Israel-Hezbollah war), helped strengthen the power of Iran's satellite, the Hezbollah movement. In a way, the road from Baghdad did lead to Jerusalem, but not as the Bush administration expected it would. Instead, Bush's policies eroded U.S. power and influence, and Washington's ability to help bring peace to Israel-Palestine waned even further. This was definitively confirmed at the hastily convened conference held in Annapolis, Maryland, in November 2007, when the Bush administration tried, but failed, to use the perceived common threat from Iran as a way to encourage Israelis and Arabs to overcome their wide differences on the core issues of the Palestinian-Israeli conflict.

A Policy of Benign Neglect

Given the manifest failures of the Bush administration's policies, the new president will have a strong incentive to re-embrace a variation of the Powell approach, consistent with the policies of the first Bush and Clinton administrations. But a truly different approach is warranted. Trying to maintain a diminishing U.S. position in the Middle East by engaging in the mission impossible of resolving the local conflict there is obviously imprudent. Like other subregional conflicts that pose no direct threat to core U.S. national interests, the situation should be left to those local and regional players with direct interest in these conflicts. A U.S. policy of "benign neglect" would provide incentives for local and regional actors to assume a larger role. These entities could "manage" the situation in the short and medium term, while trying to advance plans for a long-term resolution of the dispute.

U.S. policy makers should withdraw financial assistance to the Palestinians, and phase out aid to Israel.

That process has already begun. As U.S. diplomatic power has eroded in the region, other regional players have stepped forward. The deals brokered by Egypt for an Israeli-Palestinian cease-fire, Qatar's effort to achieve a compromise between the warring factions in Lebanon, Turkey's mediation between Israel and Syria, and even Iran's aid in mediating between the warring Shiite factions in Iraq should be welcomed. The U.S. government should factor aid from regional actors into the equation as part of a long-term strategy for "constructive disengagement" from the Middle East.

Americans who continue to push for a peace settlement should recognize that the pro-peace factions in both Israeli and Palestinian societies are weak and divided; many Palestinians and Israelis are still ready to pay a high price in blood for what they regard as a fight for survival. A settlement can be possible only when the majority of Israelis and Palestinians recognize that their interests would be best served by negotiation and peaceful resolution of the conflict, and when the minority on both sides who vehemently oppose negotiations can no longer derail the peace process.

A Strategy of Constructive Disentanglement

In the meantime, many Israelis and Palestinians are interested in keeping the United States entangled in the conflict. Few seem prepared to resolve the conflict on their own. However, the U.S. government does not have to sustain the same level of involvement in the conflict that it maintained during the Cold War [a period of mistrust between the West and Communist countries, particularly the United States and the Soviet Union]. No Arab regime can present a serious threat to Israel, whose military is unchallenged in the Middle East. Considerable American military aid to Israel might have been justified in the context of the Cold War, but is unnecessary and even harmful under present conditions. U.S. policy makers should withdraw financial assistance to the Palestinians, and phase out aid to Israel. The latter step would create an incentive for Israel to reform its economy, which has become far too dependent on financial support from the United States. Removing this support would also encourage Israel to integrate itself politically and economically into the region.

Meanwhile, U.S. direct involvement in the Israeli-Palestinian conflict does not advance American national interests. Washington should reject demands to internationalize the conflict between Israelis and Palestinians, which implicitly assume that the United States must be responsible for resolving it and paying the costs involved. Instead of complaining about the failure of the United States to make peace in the Middle East, and warning Americans of the dire consequences of failure, the Arab states should recognize that it is in their national interests and that of the long-term stability of the region to do something to resolve the Israeli-Palestinian conflict in a regional context. With its geographic proximity to the Middle East, its dependence on Middle Eastern energy resources, and the large number of Arab immigrants living in major European countries, the European Union also has a clear stake in a more peaceful Middle East. U.S. policy makers should encourage the EU to take a more active role in the region. .

A decision to adopt a more low-key approach toward the Israeli-Palestinian conflict makes sense in the context of a wider U.S. strategy of "constructive disengagement" from the Middle East. Had Washington embraced such a policy at the end of the Cold War, it could have slowed or reversed the rise of anti-Americanism. Washington's repeated, high-profile failures to deliver a peace agreement spurred continuing opposition to the U.S. military presence in the region and created the environment that gave rise to the terrorist plots of 9/11.

A Change in U.S. Strategy in the Middle East

Continuing support for American policies in the Middle East, even in the face of the obvious risks and dubious benefits, stems from the erroneous belief that American military involvement in the Middle East protects U.S. access to "cheap" oil. The notion that U.S. policy in the Middle East helps give Americans access to affordable oil makes little sense if one takes account of the military and other costs—including two Gulf wars—that should be added to the price that U.S. consumers pay for driving.

Many Americans assume that the oil resources in the Persian Gulf would be shut off if American troops were removed from the region. But the U.S. military need not be present in the Persian Gulf to ensure that the region's oil makes it to market. The oil-producing states have few resources other than oil, and if they don't sell it to somebody, they will have little wealth to maintain their power and curb domestic challenges. They need to sell oil more than the United States needs to buy it, and once this oil reaches the market, there is no practical way to somehow punish American consumers. In short, the so-called oil weapon is a dud. Further, if political and military influence were truly required to keep oil flowing, consumers in western Europe and Asia—who are far more likely than Americans to consume oil that originates in the Persian Gulf—should be the ones to bear the cost.

Reshaping U.S. policy in the Middle East would enhance American security.

Accordingly, very few economists believe that keeping U.S. troops in the region is a cost-effective strategy. During the Cold War, the U.S. policy of actively safeguarding a strategic resource may have made sense with regard to maintaining the unity of the noncommunist alliance under American leadership. At present, however, this policy is badly outdated.

A responsible policy in the Middle East, consistent with American security interests in the region, should be based on de-emphasizing U.S. alliances, especially those with Saudi Arabia and Israel. It should also include a change in popular attitudes toward U.S. dependence on Middle Eastern oil and the necessity for U.S. leadership in the negotiations to end Israeli-Palestinian conflict.

Reshaping U.S. policy in the Middle East would enhance American security and help alter the perception that U.S. policies are guided by double standards. Maintaining a frail balance among all of Washington's commitments in the region is becoming ever more costly, dangerous, and unnecessary. Americans are paying a heavy price to sustain a U.S. military and political presence there. A change is long overdue.

The United States Can No Longer Afford Military Aid to Israel

Josh Ruebner

Josh Ruebner is the national advocacy director of the US Campaign to End the Israeli Occupation, a national coalition working to change US policy toward Israel.

In his recent State of the Union address [January 25, 2010] President [Barack] Obama pledged to "go through the budget line by line to eliminate programs that we can't afford and don't work." One week later, he sent his FY2011 budget request to Congress, which included a record-breaking $3 billion in military aid to Israel.

The Cost of U.S. Weapons to Israel

This requested increase in U.S. weapons to Israel—part of a ten-year $30 billion agreement signed between the two countries in 2007—qualifies on both counts as a program that the United States can't afford and that doesn't work in establishing a just and lasting peace between Israelis and Palestinians.

Data published recently by the US Campaign to End the Israeli Occupation shows that U.S. military aid to Israel comes at a financial and moral price that this country cannot afford to pay. Its website [www.aidtoisrael.org] reveals that this same $3 billion earmark for Israel could be used instead to provide more than 364,000 low-income households with affordable housing vouchers, or to retrain 498,000 workers for green jobs, or to provide early reading programs to 887,000 at-risk students, or to provide access to primary health care services for more than 24 million uninsured Americans.

If U.S. weapons were going to Israel for a good purpose, then perhaps a coherent guns versus butter debate would be appropriate. However, Israel repeatedly misuses U.S. weapons to commit grave human rights abuses against Palestinians who are forced to live under its illegal 42-year military occupation of the West Bank, East Jerusalem, and Gaza Strip.

A Misuse of U.S. Weapons

During the [George W.] Bush administration, Israel killed at least 3,107 innocent Palestinian civilians, according to the Israeli human rights organization B'Tselem. Israel also injured thousands more innocent Palestinians and destroyed billions of dollars of Palestinian civilian infrastructure including homes, schools, factories, government buildings, and even Palestine's only airport. The severity and scale of this killing and destruction were made possible by hi-tech U.S. weapons provided to Israel at taxpayer expense.

And during Obama's first year in office, Israel continued to misuse its stock of U.S. weapons to entrench its apartheid policies toward Palestinians by maintaining its illegal blockade of the Gaza Strip—collectively punishing its 1.5 million Palestinian residents by severely restricting the flow of humanitarian relief—and building illegal Israeli-only colonies on stolen Palestinian land in the West Bank and East Jerusalem.

It was exactly to prevent this kind of misuse of U.S. weapons that Congress passed the Arms Export Control Act, which strictly limits foreign countries from employing U.S. weapons for any purpose other than "internal security" or "legitimate self-defense." Building apartheid walls and colonies to maintain a foreign military occupation, enforcing a medieval blockade, and killing and injuring innocent civilians by the thousands certainly cannot be considered legitimate and is self-evidently not for domestic security.

Yet despite this clear misuse of U.S. weapons by Israel— most evident recently during its December 2008–January 2009 attack on the Gaza Strip which killed more than 1,300 Palestinians in just three weeks—both Congress and the Obama administration have failed miserably to hold Israel accountable for its violations of the Arms Export Control Act and cut off weapons flow to it as required by the law.

The President's Lack of Response

A few lonely voices on Capitol Hill—such as Rep. Brian Baird, Rep. Keith Ellison, and Rep. Dennis Kucinich—have spoken up bravely and truthfully about the consequences of U.S. weapons transferred to Israel, which a 2009 Amnesty International report cited as literally "fuelling" the Israeli-Palestinian conflict.

Unfortunately, President Obama has paid no heed to these members of Congress. When questioned at a recent town hall meeting in Tampa about the impact of U.S. military aid to Israel on Palestinian civilians, the normally articulate Obama appeared visibly flummoxed before sputtering, "Look, look, look, the Middle East is obviously an issue that has plagued the region for centuries." He then proceeded to duck the question with platitudes about peace.

The president's nonresponse to the question demonstrates that politicians prefer to turn a blind eye to the obvious incompatibility of trying to promote Israeli-Palestinian peace while giving Israel the weapons it needs to maintain its illegal occupation of Palestinian lands.

Before Congress gets to work on the president's budget request and considers transferring an additional $3 billion in weapons to Israel, it is long past overdue for the United States to reconsider whether we can afford this policy any longer.

The United States Should Not Pursue Military Strikes or Regime Change in Iran

Christopher Hemmer

Christopher Hemmer is professor and deputy chair in the Department of International Security Studies at the Air War College, a part of the US Air Force's Air University.

W hat should American foreign policy be if current efforts to discourage Iran from developing nuclear weapons fail? Despite the recent resumption of high-level contacts between Iran and the International Atomic Energy Agency, and the potential for stronger action by the United Nations Security Council, an Iranian nuclear weapon remains a distinct possibility. The current debate regarding US policy toward Iran revolves around the relative merits of a preventive military strike, including the possibility of seeking regime change in Tehran [Iran's capital], versus a policy that focuses on diplomacy and economic sanctions to dissuade Iran from pursuing a nuclear bomb. This debate, however, risks prematurely foreclosing discussions regarding a wide range of foreign policy options should diplomacy and sanctions fail to persuade Tehran to limit its nuclear ambitions.

The choices America would face if Iran developed nuclear weapons are not simply between preventive military action and doing nothing. The calculations America would face are not between the costs of action versus the costs of inaction. A nuclear-armed Iran will certainly pose a number of challenges for the United States. Those challenges, however, can be met through an active policy of deterrence, containment, engagement, and the reassurance of America's allies in the region.

Christopher Hemmer, "Responding to a Nuclear Iran," *Parameters*, vol. 37, no. 3, Autumn 2007, pp. 42–53. www.carlisle.army.mil.

American Interests in the Persian Gulf

The United States has three strategic interests in the Persian Gulf: maintaining the flow of oil onto world markets, preventing any hostile state from dominating the region, and minimizing any terrorist threat. Given these interests, the challenges posed by a nuclear-armed Iran need to be addressed by a policy that minimizes the threat to key oil production and transportation infrastructure and negates any Iranian bid for regional hegemony. Additionally, any action taken toward Iran has to be weighed against the potential impact it may have with regard to the global war on terrorism and ongoing US initiatives related to nation building in Iraq and Afghanistan. Moreover, such a policy needs to be executed in a manner that avoids any nuclear threat to the United States or its allies.

The end-state the United States should be working toward, as a result of these strategic interests, is an Iran that is an integral part of the global economy, at peace with its neighbors, and not supportive of terrorist organizations. While America's strategic interests do not include the proliferation of democracy, any acceptable end-state will likely require some measure of democratic reform. Given the fact that anti-Americanism and anti-Zionism are an integral part of the Islamic republic's identity, some measure of regime evolution will be required in an effort to advance America's long-term interests.

The Perils of a Preventive Strike

Any attempt to disarm Iran through the use of military options would in all likelihood damage America's interests in the region. While a military option might inflict significant damage on Iran's infrastructure by damaging or destroying its nuclear weapons program, disrupting its regional ambitions, and possibly serving as a deterrent to future proliferators, the likely costs would far outweigh the benefits.

First, any military action against Iran would send seismic shocks through global energy markets at a time when the price of oil is already at record highs. Since Iran relies heavily on the income derived from oil exports, it is unlikely that it would withhold petroleum from global markets. Iran may, however, threaten to disrupt the flow of traffic through the Strait of Hormuz or sponsor attacks on key oil infrastructure on the territory of America's Gulf allies. Such actions could hurt the US economy and potentially bolster Iranian revenue by raising the price of oil. While it is true that the world market would eventually adjust to such actions, as [journalist] James Fallows has noted, that is a bit like saying eventually the US stock market adjusted to the Great Depression.

Any direct military action against Iran could also have a significant impact on America's war on terrorism. Such action would only serve to confirm many of Osama bin Laden's statements that the United States is at war with the world of Islam. This charge would be difficult to counter, given the fact that the United States has looked the other way for years with regard to Israel's nuclear program, accepted India as a legitimate nuclear state, and is negotiating with North Korea regarding its nuclear ambitions.

Any military action against Iran would also undermine America's nation-building efforts in Iraq and Afghanistan, due to possible Iranian retaliation in both countries. While Iranian efforts toward stabilizing these two states have been sporadic at best, and purposively obstructive at worst, there is little reason to doubt that Iran could make achieving US objectives in Iraq and Afghanistan far more difficult. Although mostly bluster, there is some truth to former Iranian President Ali Rafsanjani's argument that as long as American troops maintain a formidable presence on Iran's borders, "it is the United States that is besieged by Iran." The same holds true regarding Iran's ties to Hezbollah and its presence in Lebanon. By targeting Iran's nuclear program the United States would unwisely encourage Iranian escalation in a number of these arenas.

Military strikes against Tehran would also undermine Washington's long-term goal of seeing reform movements succeed in Iran. If the history of military incursions and the Iranian nation teach us anything it is the fact that intervention is likely to solidify support for the current regime. The idea that the Iranian people would react to a military strike by advocating the overthrow of the existing regime is delusional. Instead the likely outcome of any direct military incursion would be the bolstering of the current regime.

The reason a policy advocating regime change is a bad idea, given its potential benefits, is the fact that such a policy is beyond America's means.

Moreover, any preventive attack, no matter how effective, is only a temporary fix. First, such a campaign will eliminate only that portion of Iran's nuclear program known to intelligence agencies. Even after the extensive bombing campaign of the 1990–1991 Gulf War, subsequent inspections discovered large parts of Iraq's unconventional weapons programs that were previously unknown. More importantly, even if such an attack succeeded in eliminating significant facets of Iran's nuclear program, it would do little toward discouraging Iran from rebuilding those assets. Thus, even after a fully successful denial campaign, the United States, in a number of years, would likely face the prospect of having to do it all over again.

The Problem with Regime Change

Given the limits of any preventive strike, perhaps the United States should not restrict its goal in Iran to simply nuclear disarmament, but opt instead for the broader objective of regime change. If successful, regime change in Iran could provide for a number of benefits. It may eliminate the Iranian threat of interrupting the flow of oil from the region; it would also send a strong message to potential proliferators about the costs of similar actions; it might diminish Iran's support for terrorism; even possibly eliminate the threat of official Iranian meddling in Iraq and Afghanistan; and could potentially curtail Iran's nuclear ambitions.

The reason a policy advocating regime change is a bad idea, given its potential benefits, is the fact that such a policy is beyond America's means. While the United States certainly possesses the capability to eliminate the regime in Tehran, as the invasion of Iraq has shown, eliminating the present leadership is the easy part of regime change. The more difficult and costly challenge is installing a new government. With America's resources already overly committed in Afghanistan and Iraq, taking on a new nation-building mission in a country far larger and in some ways far more nationalistic than Iraq would be the epitome of strategic overreach.

Additionally, one of the few scenarios where Iran might use its nuclear capability would be if Tehran believed that the United States intended to exercise forcible regime change. A nuclear strike against any American presence in the region might be seen by the leadership in Tehran as its last hope for survival. It goes without saying that once any government has crossed the nuclear threshold, forcible regime change by an external actor is no longer a viable option. The threat of nuclear retaliation would simply be too great. Indeed, this is probably the most important reason why states such as Iran and North Korea desire nuclear weapons. Does this mean that the United States should therefore seek regime change before Iran develops its nuclear capability? No; even without nuclear weapons, forcible regime change in Iran and the ensuing occupation would entail too great a commitment of resources on the part of the United States. Pursuing regime change in Iran as a response to its nuclear program would be akin to treating a brain tumor with a guillotine. The proposed cure is worse than the disease.

Fortunately, US policy options for dealing with a nuclear Iran are not limited to preventive military strikes, regime change, or doing nothing. A more promising option would have four key components. First, deter Iran from ever using its nuclear weapons. Second, prevent Iran from using its nuclear status to increase its influence in the region. Third, engage Iran in a meaningful way that encourages the creation of a government friendly to the United States and its regional allies, one that does not sponsor terrorism. Finally, such a policy should reassure US allies in the region that America's commitment to their security is steadfast. This four-pronged strategy would do a better job of protecting American interests in the region than any military strike or forcible regime change.

Iranian leaders are rational enough to understand that any use of nuclear weapons against the United States or its allies would result in an overwhelming and unacceptable response.

The Strategy of Nuclear Deterrence

America's overriding concern regarding Iran's nuclear weapons program is that these weapons are never used against the United States or its allies. Fortunately, the strategy of nuclear deterrence can go a long way in resolving this problem. The threat of annihilation as the result of an American retaliatory strike can be a powerful deterrent. As the United States and the Soviet Union discovered during the Cold War [a period of mistrust between the West and Communist countries, particularly the United States and the Soviet Union] and as India and Pakistan have recently learned, the threat of nuclear retaliation makes the use of such weapons problematic.

The central question in any debate over America's policies toward a nuclear Iran is whether or not the regime in Tehran is deterrable. If in fact it is, then deterrence is a less costly and risky strategy than prevention. Proponents of the preventive use of military force argue, as did the alarmists in the late 1940s with regard to the Soviet Union and in the early 1960s about China, that Iran is a revolutionary state seeking to export its destabilizing ideology. For these analysts Iran is often depicted as a regime of religious zealots that cannot be deterred because they are willing to accept an apocalyptic end to any conflict.

While Iran's track record with regard to its foreign policy does indicate a regime that is hostile to America, nothing would indicate that Iran is beyond the realm of nuclear deterrence. The bulk of the revolutionary fervor demonstrated by the Islamic republic during its infancy died during the long war with Iraq. Moreover, the power of nuclear deterrence lies in the fact that precise calculations and cost and benefit analyses are not needed given the overwhelming costs associated with any nuclear exchange. Iranian leaders are rational enough to understand that any use of nuclear weapons against the United States or its allies would result in an overwhelming and unacceptable response. . . .

A Policy of Containment

The second pillar of US strategy toward a nuclear Iran should be a policy of containment, to be certain that Iran does not succeed in exercising its nuclear capability as a tool of coercive diplomacy against US or allied interests in the region. Given Iran's perception of itself as the historically preeminent power in the region, Tehran can be expected to continue its policy attempting to increase its regional influence at the expense of the United States.

How would the possession of a deliverable nuclear weapon impact Tehran's foreign policy agenda? One possibility is that a nuclear Iran might be more, rather than less, restrained in its regional agenda. If any of Iran's actions are driven by a sense of insecurity with regard to America's intentions (or the threat created by a nuclear Pakistan or Israel, even the possibility of a resurgent Iraq), the security that Tehran would gain from having its own nuclear deterrent could make the nation's leadership less worried about the regional balance of power. Moreover, possession of a nuclear weapon would certainly increase the attention other world powers paid Iran. The leadership in Tehran would have to continually worry that if any crisis developed involving another nuclear power the potential foe might opt for a preemptive attack on Iranian nuclear facilities. The fear that even a limited conflict might escalate into a nuclear exchange could make Tehran more cautious across the entire spectrum of conflict.

Washington would be better served by engaging Iran rather than attempting to isolate it.

While such pressures may play a limited role in Iran's decision making, it would be unwise for the United States to put too much faith in such possibilities. First, Iran's regional behavior is only partially driven by security fears. Even if Iran believed there was no threat from the United States, its status as a potential regional hegemon gives it incentive to increase its role in regional affairs. Second, while a limited amount of learning related to nuclear crisis management did take place during the Cold War, it took the United States and the Soviets a number of crises to fully appreciate these lessons. Although the existence of this Cold War record might enable Iran to learn such lessons more quickly, the limits of vicarious learning offer ample reasons to doubt that Iran will internalize these dictums without experiencing similar crises.

The result is that Iran can probably be expected to continue furthering its regional agenda in an attempt to increase its stature and diminish that of the United States. At least initially, any increased nuclear capability will likely embolden rather than induce caution on the part of Iran's leadership.

Having gone to great lengths and paid significant costs to develop its nuclear capabilities, Iran is likely to continue testing the regional and international waters. Such efforts are bound to create challenges for the United States and its allies. The good news is that nuclear weapons have proven to be poor tools for coercive diplomacy, especially against states that already possess nuclear weapons or who may be allied with a nuclear power. Nuclear weapons have proven to be extraordinarily effective at two tasks: deterring the use of such weapons against other nuclear powers or their allies, and deterring states from directly challenging the vital interests of a nuclear power. Beyond these two critical tasks, however, nuclear weapons have not proven particularly useful as diplomatic tools of intimidation. For the United States and its allies, a policy of containment against Iranian attempts to expand its influence in the region is the correct foreign policy strategy. Certainly, such a strategy far outweighs any policy based on preventive war.

A Policy of Engagement

To advance America's long-range goal of an Iran that is part of the global economy, at peace with its neighbors, and not supporting terrorism, Washington would be better served by engaging Iran rather than attempting to isolate it. A policy of engagement could take two forms: the establishment of direct diplomatic relations and the encouragement of Iran's involvement in the global economy.

The United States broke diplomatic ties with Iran in April 1980, during the hostage crisis [when Iranian militants took over the US embassy in Tehran and held fifty-two American citizens hostage for more than a year]. The establishment of direct diplomatic ties between the United States and Iran, however, should not be seen as any form of a reward to Iran or as approval of Iranian policies. Nor should the reestablishment of formal relations be seen as the final stage in some sort of grand bargain. Instead, diplomatic relations should be viewed as part of the normal business of conducting America's foreign policy. There is little reason to doubt that Iran would portray any US initiative to reestablish diplomatic relations as a victory, as Tehran did with the recent moves by the Bush administration to engage in direct talks related to the situation in Iraq. America should not let fear of such a reaction stand in the way of any initiative that would advance America's long-term security interests.

Over the years the United States has found that it needs diplomatic relations with hostile states as well as with allies. Such relationships were maintained throughout the Cold War with the Soviet Union, despite numerous crises and conflicts. In the case of Iran the absence of direct governmental links makes it more difficult to deter and contain Iran. Obviously, Iran would have to concur in the reestablishment of any form of diplomatic relations.

America's most promising strategy toward a nuclear-armed Iran should be the development of a security architecture based on deterrence and containment.

Given the number of domestic challenges the Islamic republic is facing, most notably a tremendous growth in its youthful population, combined with the incompetence and corruption that has marked its stewardship of the Iranian economy, it is hard to imagine that this regime can continue to avoid collapse without significant reform. At the same time, there is little reason to expect that a democratic revolution is imminent. The reform movements that seemed so promising in the late 1990s have largely been defeated. The best strategy for revitalizing these movements is to encourage Tehran's involvement in the world economy, as opposed to further attempts at isolation. Increasing the Iranian people's exposure to the world economy is much more likely to increase motivation and expand the resources available to any future reform movement. Iran's eventual inclusion in the World Trade Organization is one of the carrots currently being held out to Iran as part of ongoing negotiations regarding its nuclear program. Such incentives may advance America's long-term foreign policy goals in the region even if those efforts fail to negate Iran's development of a nuclear weapon. . . .

Reassure Iran's Neighbors

The final portion of a US strategy toward a nuclear-armed Iran should focus on convincing Iran's neighbors that the American commitment to their security remains strong. If the United States wants regional powers to resist Iranian attempts at expanding its influence, then Washington needs to bolster security ties in the region. Improving security cooperation with Iran's neighbors could advance a number of American interests beyond simple containment. Such efforts could also help increase the security of the oil infrastructure in the region, as well as expand intelligence cooperation related to international terrorism.

A more definite US security commitment to Iran's neighbors may also decrease the chance that the development of a nuclear weapon would increase the threat of nuclear proliferation in the region. Egypt, Turkey, and Saudi Arabia have been cited as states likely to respond to any Iranian nuclear capability with increased nuclear programs. Egypt, however, has been able to tolerate a nuclear Israel for more than 30 years, as well as accommodate Libya's weapons programs. Given that historical precedent, it is unlikely that an Iranian bomb would dramatically change Cairo's calculations. Similarly, Turkey's membership in the North Atlantic Treaty Organization and its desire to join the European Union are likely to dissuade Ankara [the capital of Turkey] from attempting to join the nuclear fraternity. Saudi Arabia and the other members of the Gulf Cooperation Council, however, would more than likely attempt to strengthen security ties with the United States in an effort to bolster their position against a nuclear Iran.

Part of America's strategy regarding regional allies needs to focus on assuring individual states that as long as Iran is contained, the United States will not take any preventive military action. While the Gulf States certainly would prefer that Iran not develop nuclear weapons, it is also important to recognize that they fear any US-Iranian conflict more than they fear the prospect of a nuclear Iran. America's most promising strategy toward a nuclear-armed Iran should be the development of a security architecture based on deterrence and containment.

Organizations to Contact

The editors have compiled the following list of organizations concerned with the issues debated in this book. The descriptions are derived from materials provided by the organizations. All have publications or information available for interested readers. The list was compiled on the date of publication of the present volume; names, addresses, phone and fax numbers, and e-mail and Internet addresses may change. Be aware that many organizations take several weeks or longer to respond to inquiries, so allow as much time as possible.

American Foreign Policy Council (AFPC)
509 C Street NE, Washington, DC 20002
(202) 543-1006 • fax: (202) 543-1007
e-mail: afpc@afpc.org
website: www.afpc.org

The American Foreign Policy Council (AFPC) is a nonprofit organization dedicated to bringing information to those who make or influence the foreign policy of the United States. AFPC provides resources to members of Congress, the executive branch, and the policy-making community. AFPC publishes policy papers and numerous in-house bulletins, including *Iran Democracy Monitor*.

American Israel Public Affairs Committee (AIPAC)
251 H Street NW, Washington, DC 20001
(202) 639-5200 • fax: (202) 347-4918
website: www.aipac.org

The American Israel Public Affairs Committee (AIPAC) is a pro-Israel lobby that works to strengthen the US-Israeli relationship. AIPAC works with both Democratic and Republican political leaders to enact public policy that supports Israel.

Among its publications are *Near East Report, Defense Digest*, and issue memos such as "Foreign Aid: Keeping America Safe, Strong, and Prosperous."

Brookings Institution
1775 Massachusetts Avenue NW, Washington, DC   20036
(202) 797-6000
e-mail: communications@brookings.edu
website: www.brookings.edu

The Brookings Institution is a nonprofit public policy organization that conducts independent research. The Brookings Institution uses its research, including that conducted by the Saban Center for Middle East Policy, to provide recommendations that advance the goals of strengthening American democracy, fostering social welfare and security, and securing a cooperative international system. The Brookings Institution publishes its research in multiple venues, including titles such as *Generation in Waiting*, a book published by Brookings Institution Press.

Cato Institute
1000 Massachusetts Avenue NW
Washington, DC   20001-5403
(202) 842-0200 • fax: (202) 842-3490
website: www.cato.org

The Cato Institute is a public policy research foundation dedicated to limiting the role of government, protecting individual liberties, and promoting free markets. The Cato Institute works to originate, advocate, promote, and disseminate applicable policy proposals that create free, open, and civil societies in the United States and throughout the world. Among the Cato Institute's many publications are the *Cato Journal* and the bimonthly *Cato Policy Report*.

Center for Strategic & International Studies (CSIS)
1800 K Street NW, Washington, DC   20006
(202) 887-0200 • fax: (202) 775-3199
website: www.csis.org

The Center for Strategic & International Studies (CSIS) is a nonprofit organization that provides strategic insights and bipartisan policy solutions to decision makers. CSIS conducts research and analysis for decision makers in government, international institutions, the private sector, and civil society. Among its many publications are the reports "Stability in the Middle East and North Africa: The Other Side of Security" and "The Egyptian Military and the Arab-Israeli Military Balance," both available at its website.

Council on Foreign Relations (CFR)
The Harold Pratt House, 58 East Sixty-eighth Street
New York, NY   10065
(212) 434-9400 • fax: (212) 434-9800
e-mail: communications@cfr.org
website: www.cfr.org

The Council on Foreign Relations (CFR) is an independent, nonpartisan membership organization, think tank, and publisher. CFR aims to be a resource for its members, government officials, business executives, journalists, educators and students, civic and religious leaders, and other interested citizens to help them better understand the world and the foreign policy choices facing the United States and other countries. CFR has numerous publications available at its website, including the journal *Foreign Affairs*, backgrounders, expert briefs, and testimony such as the recent "Egypt, Lebanon, and US Policy in the Middle East" by a senior fellow of the council.

Foreign Policy Research Institute (FPRI)
1528 Walnut Street, Suite 610, Philadelphia, PA   19102
(215) 732-3774 • fax: (215) 732-4401
e-mail: fpri@fpri.org
website: www.fpri.org

The Foreign Policy Research Institute (FPRI) is an independent, nonprofit organization devoted to bringing the insights of scholarship to bear on the development of policies that advance US national interests. FPRI conducts research on pressing issues and provides public education on international affairs. The organization publishes the quarterly *Orbis*, several periodical bulletins, and numerous essays, all of which are available at its website.

Foundation for Middle East Peace (FMEP)

1761 N Street NW, Washington, DC   20036
(202) 835-3650 • fax: (202) 835-3651
e-mail: info@fmep.org
website: www.fmep.org

The Foundation for Middle East Peace (FMEP) is a nonprofit organization that promotes peace between Israel and Palestine, via two states, meeting the fundamental needs of both peoples. FMEP offers speakers, sponsors programs, and makes small grants in pursuit of this peace. FMEP publishes the *Report on Israeli Settlement in the Occupied Territories* containing analysis, commentary, maps, and other data on the Israeli-Palestinian conflict.

Institute for Palestine Studies (IPS)

3501 M Street NW, Washington, DC   20007
(202) 342-3990 • fax: (202) 342-3927
e-mail: ipsdc@palestine-studies.org
website: www.palestine-studies.org

The Institute for Palestine Studies (IPS) is a global institute that aims to protect the integrity of the historical record on the Arab-Israeli conflict. IPS is exclusively devoted to documentation, research, analysis, and publication on Palestinian affairs and the Arab-Israeli conflict. IPS publishes *Journal of Palestine Studies, Jerusalem Quarterly*, and *Quarterly Update on Conflict and Diplomacy*.

Middle East Forum

1500 Walnut Street, Suite 1050, Philadelphia, PA   19102
(215) 546-5406 • fax: (215) 546-5409

e-mail: info@meforum.org
website: www.meforum.org

The Middle East Forum works to promote American interests in the Middle East and to protect the US constitutional order from Middle Eastern threats. The Middle East Forum combats lawful Islamism; protects the freedom of public speech of anti-Islamist authors, activists, and publishers; and works to improve Middle East studies in North America. The Middle East Forum publishes the journal *Middle East Quarterly* and publishes articles through its program Islamist Watch.

Middle East Institute (MEI)

1761 N Street NW, Washington, DC 20036-2882
(202) 785-1141 • fax: (202) 331-8861
e-mail: information@mei.edu
website: www.mei.edu

The Middle East Institute (MEI) is dedicated solely to the study of the Middle East. MEI sponsors conferences, instructs students, provides materials through the George Camp Keiser Library, and hosts scholars. MEI publishes the *Middle East Journal* and several web publications, including *Policy Briefs, Commentaries, Viewpoints,* and *Encounters.*

Middle East Policy Council

1730 M Street NW, Suite 512, Washington, DC 20036
(202) 296-6767 • fax: (202) 296-5791
e-mail: info@mepc.org
website: www.mepc.org

The Middle East Policy Council is a nonprofit organization whose mission is to contribute to American understanding of the political, economic, and cultural issues that affect US interests in the Middle East. The Middle East Policy Council conducts the Capitol Hill Conference series for policy makers and their staffs to offer multiple points of view on complex issues and offers professional-development workshops for K–12 educators. The Middle East Policy Council publishes the quarterly journal *Middle East Policy* and provides other articles and commentary at its website.

National Council on US-Arab Relations

1730 M Street NW, Suite 503, Washington, DC   20036
(202) 293-6466 • fax: (202) 293-7770
website: www.ncusar.org

The National Council on US-Arab Relations is a nonprofit, nongovernmental, educational organization dedicated to improving American knowledge and understanding of the Arab world. The National Council on US-Arab Relations promotes leadership development, people-to-people exchanges, lectures, an annual Arab-US policy makers conference, and the participation of American students and faculty in Arab study experiences. It provides videos, podcasts, and other commentary at its website, including the article "War with Iran: Regional Reactions and Requirements."

Washington Institute for Near East Policy

1828 L Street NW, Suite 1050, Washington, DC   20036
(202) 452-0650 • fax: (202) 223-5364
website: www.washingtoninstitute.org

The Washington Institute for Near East Policy was established to advance a balanced and realistic understanding of American interests in the Middle East. The institute promotes an American engagement in the Middle East committed to strengthening alliances, nurturing friendships, and promoting security, peace, prosperity, and democracy for the people of the region. The Washington Institute for Near East Policy publishes a variety of analysis available at its website, including the article "If War Comes: Israel vs. Hizballah and Its Allies," which can be found in the journal *PolicyWatch*.

Bibliography

Books

Ali Abunimah   *One Country: A Bold Proposal to End
                    the Israeli-Palestinian Impasse*. New
                    York: Metropolitan Books, 2006.

Phyllis Bennis   *Understanding the Palestinian-Israeli
                    Conflict: A Primer*. Northampton,
                    MA: Olive Branch Press, 2007.

Peter L. Bergen   *The Longest War: The Enduring
                    Conflict Between America and al-
                    Qaeda*. New York: Free Press, 2011.

John Bolton   *Surrender Is Not an Option:
                    Defending America at the United
                    Nations and Abroad*. New York:
                    Threshold Editions, 2008.

Edmund Burke   *Struggle and Survival in the Modern
III and David N.   Middle East*. Berkeley: University of
Yaghoubian, eds.   California Press, 2006.

Ann Chamberlin   *A History of Women's Seclusion in the
                    Middle East: The Veil in the Looking
                    Glass*. New York: Haworth Press,
                    2006.

Alan Dershowitz   *The Case for Peace: How the
                    Arab-Israeli Conflict Can Be Resolved*.
                    Hoboken, NJ: John Wiley, 2005.

Peter W.
Galbraith
The End of Iraq: How American Incompetence Created a War Without End. New York: Simon & Schuster, 2006.

Stephen Kinzer
All the Shah's Men: An American Coup and the Roots of Middle East Terror. Hoboken, NJ: John Wiley & Sons, 2008.

Joel Kovel
Overcoming Zionism: Creating a Single Democratic State in Israel/Palestine. Ann Arbor, MI: Pluto, 2007.

Timur Kuran
The Long Divergence: How Islamic Law Held Back the Middle East. Princeton, NJ: Princeton University Press, 2011.

Joseph Massad
The Persistence of the Palestinian Question: Essays on Zionism and the Palestinians. New York: Routledge, 2006.

John J.
Mearsheimer and
Stephen M. Walt
The Israel Lobby and U.S. Foreign Policy. New York: Farrar, Straus, and Giroux, 2008.

Tarek Osman
Egypt on the Brink: From Nasser to Mubarak. New Haven, CT: Yale University Press, 2010.

Walid Phares
The Coming Revolution: Struggle for Freedom in the Middle East. New York: Threshold Editions, 2010.

Kenneth M. Pollack
A Path Out of the Desert: A Grand Strategy for America in the Middle East. New York: Random House, 2009.

Thomas E. Ricks
Fiasco: The American Military Adventure in Iraq. New York: Penguin Press, 2006.

Jacqueline Rose
The Question of Zion. Princeton, NJ: Princeton University Press, 2005.

Joel C. Rosenberg
Inside the Revolution. Carol Stream, IL: Tyndale House Publishers, 2009.

Dan Senor and Saul Singer
Start-Up Nation: The Story of Israel's Economic Miracle. New York: Twelve, 2009.

Michael Sorkin, ed.
Against the Wall: Israeli's Barrier to Peace. New York: New Press, 2005.

Periodicals and Internet Sources

David Axe, Malou Innocent, and Jason Reich
"Defining Victory to Win a War," *Foreign Policy*, October 6, 2009.

Andrew J. Bacevich and Matthew A. Shadle
"No Exit from Iraq?" *Commonweal*, October 12, 2007.

Roi Ben-Yehuda
"Bring Hamas to the Table," *The Daily Beast*, September 4, 2010. www.thedailybeast.com.

Ilan Berman   "The Case for Economic Warfare," *Iran Strategy Brief*, January 2008. www.afpc.org.

John Bolton   "The Case for Striking Iran Grows," *Wall Street Journal*, February 11, 2010.

Christopher Boucek   "Yemen's Problems Will Not Stay in Yemen," CNN.com, December 30, 2009. www.cnn.com.

Daniel Byman   "How to Handle Hamas," *Foreign Affairs*, September–October 2010.

Anthony H. Cordesman   "Iraq: 'Mission Accomplished' Mark II," Center for Strategic & International Studies, August 20, 2010. www.csis.org.

Newt Gingrich   "President Obama and Congress Must Stop Iran's Nuclear Program," *Politico*, May 19, 2010.

Leon T. Hadar   "Victory in Iraq at Last (Not!)," *Huffington Post*, March 9, 2010.

Shadi Hamid   "Arab Elections: Free, Sort of Fair . . . and Meaningless," *Foreign Policy*, October 27, 2010.

David Harris   "Palestinian Leaders: Denying Reality, Delaying Peace," *Huffington Post*, October 12, 2010.

Arthur Herman   "Al Qaeda on the Rise," *New York Post*, October 20, 2010.

Martin S. Indyk   "For Once, Hope in the Middle East," *New York Times*, August 26, 2010.

Chalmers Johnson   "America's Unwelcome Advances," *Mother Jones*, August 22, 2008.

Frederick W. Kagan and Christopher Harnisch   "How to Apply 'Smart Power' in Yemen," *Wall Street Journal*, January 14, 2010.

Robert Kagan   "How Obama Can Reverse Iran's Dangerous Course," *Washington Post*, January 27, 2010.

Rashid Khalidi   "Bad Faith in the Holy City," *Foreign Affairs*, April 15, 2010.

Christopher Layne   "Balancing Act: The U.S. Could Be More Secure by Doing Less," *American Conservative*, September 10, 2007.

Mark R. Levin   "Not So Fast," *National Review Online*, September 4, 2009. www.nationalreview.com.

Jane C. Loeffler   "Fortress America," *Foreign Policy*, August 15, 2007.

Andrew C. McCarthy   "A Dangerous Delusion," *National Review Online*, September 4, 2009. www.nationalreview.com.

Robert W. McElroy   "Why We Must Withdraw from Iraq," *America*, April 30, 2007.

Ahmed Moor "The Case for a One-State Solution," *Huffington Post*, April 20, 2010.

Joshua Muravchik "Bomb Iran," *Los Angeles Times*, November 19, 2006.

Danielle Pletka "Iran Sanctions Are Failing. What's Next?" *Wall Street Journal*, March 31, 2010.

Norman Podhoretz "The Case for Bombing Iran," *Commentary*, June 2007.

Kenneth M. Pollack "Deterring a Nuclear Iran: The Devil in the Details," Council on Foreign Relations, June 2010. www.cfr.org.

Christopher Preble "Time to Leave," *USA Today*, December 2, 2009.

Dmitry Reider "Who's Afraid of a One-State Solution?" *Foreign Policy*, March 31, 2010.

Bruce Riedel "If Israel Attacks," *National Interest*, September–October 2010.

Michael Rubin "Sanctioning Iran," *Weekly Standard*, November 8, 2010.

Bilal Y. Saab "The Israeli-Palestinian Conflict: Beyond Gaza," *World Today*, February 2009.

Robert Scheer "Two Wars Don't Make a Right," *Nation*, September 1, 2010.

Bret Stephens "Iran Cannot Be Contained," *Commentary*, July–August 2010.

Erik Swabb   "The US Needs to Stay in Iraq,"
Boston Globe, March 20, 2007.

Charlie Szrom   "Our Enemies Have a Strategy. Do
We?" *National Review Online*,
November 1, 2010.
www.nationalreview.com.

Shibley Telhami   "Can Obama Please Both Arabs and
Israelis?" *Foreign Policy*, August 25,
2010.

Paul D. Wolfowitz "In Korea, a Model for Iraq," *New
York Times*, August 30, 2010.

Index